29 World Bank Discussion Papers

A Multisector Framework for Analysis of Stabilization and Structural Adjustment Policies

The Case of Morocco

Abel Mateus and others

The World Bank
Washington, D.C.

Copyright © 1988
The World Bank
1818 H Street, N.W.
Washington, D.C. 20433, U.S.A.

All rights reserved
Manufactured in the United States of America
First printing June 1988

Discussion Papers are not formal publications of the World Bank. They present preliminary and unpolished results of country analysis or research that is circulated to encourage discussion and comment; citation and the use of such a paper should take account of its provisional character. The findings, interpretations, and conclusions expressed in this paper are entirely those of the author(s) and should not be attributed in any manner to the World Bank, to its affiliated organizations, or to members of its Board of Executive Directors or the countries they represent. Any maps that accompany the text have been prepared solely for the convenience of readers; the designations and presentation of material in them do not imply the expression of any opinion whatsoever on the part of the World Bank, its affiliates, or its Board or member countries concerning the legal status of any country, territory, city, or area or of the authorities thereof or concerning the delimitation of its boundaries or its national affiliation.

Because of the informality and to present the results of research with the least possible delay, the typescript has not been prepared in accordance with the procedures appropriate to formal printed texts, and the World Bank accepts no responsibility for errors.

The material in this publication is copyrighted. Requests for permission to reproduce portions of it should be sent to Director, Publications Department at the address shown in the copyright notice above. The World Bank encourages dissemination of its work and will normally give permission promptly and, when the reproduction is for noncommercial purposes, without asking a fee. Permission to photocopy portions for classroom use is not required, though notification of such use having been made will be appreciated.

The most recent World Bank publications are described in the catalog *New Publications*, a new edition of which is issued in the spring and fall of each year. The complete backlist of publications is shown in the annual *Index of Publications*, which contains an alphabetical title list and indexes of subjects, authors, and countries and regions; it is of value principally to libraries and institutional purchasers. The latest edition of each of these is available free of charge from Publications Sales Unit, Department F, The World Bank, 1818 H Street, N.W., Washington, D.C. 20433, U.S.A., or from Publications, The World Bank, 66, avenue d'Iéna, 75116 Paris, France.

Abel Mateus is a senior economist in the Europe, Middle East, and North Africa Regional Office of the World Bank.

Library of Congress Cataloging-in-Publication Data

```
Mateus, Abel Moreira.
   A multisector framework for analysis of stabilization and
 structural adjustment policies : the case of Morocco / Abel Mateus
 and others.
      p.   cm. -- (World Bank discussion papers ; 29)
   Includes bibliographical references.
   ISBN 0-8213-1071-2
   1. Morocco--Economic policy--Econometric models.  2. Economic
 stabilization--Morocco--Econometric models.  3. Equilibrium
 (Economics)--Econometric models.   I. Title. II. Series.
 HC810.M38 1988
 339.5'0964--dc19                                            88-14713
                                                                 CIP
```

FOREWORD

This project was carried out by and under the direction of Abel Mateus. We would like to thank J. Shilling and A. Stoutjesdijk at the World Bank, and M. Bijad and M. Tadili in the Ministry of Planning in Morocco for all their support to the project. In the formulation of the model, he collaborated with Clive Bell (DRD, World Bank). In the construction of the Social Accounting Matrix, formulation of the computer program and the initial calibration, he had the collaboration of Elizabeth Sadoulet (consultant, University of California at Berkeley) and A. Drud (DRD, World Bank). We acknowledge the efficient assistance of Sylvie Morin in the estimation of the demand system and of S. Pal in general research assistance.

TABLE OF CONTENTS

	Pages
PART I: THE GENERAL EQUILIBRIUM MODEL OF MOROCCO STRUCTURE, DATA AND MODEL SOLUTION	1-49
INTRODUCTION	1
CHAPTER I: BACKGROUND	4-18
1.1 Growth performance and supply side	4
1.2 Demand management	6
1.3 The 1983-85 adjustment cum-structural adjustment program	7
1.4 Incentives policies	13
1.5 Sector strategies	14
1.6 Investment policies	15
1.7 External trade strategies and openness of the economy	16
CHAPTER II: THE BASIC GENERAL EQUILIBRIUM MODEL	19-34
2.1 An overview of the basic model	19
2.2 The supply side and production structure	20
2.3 The demand side and consumption income distribution	25
2.4 Market adjustment in traded and non-traded goods market	25
2.5 Equilibrium solution for the Morocco 85 model	30
2.6 Alternative model specifications (liberalized economy model)	32
CHAPTER III: DATA BASE AND CALIBRATION	35-49
3.1 The choice of functional forms for the behavioral equations in the model	37
3.2 Alternative approaches to parameter selection	38
3.3 The construction of a benchmark equilibrium data set	40
3.4 Production function and trade elasticities	41
3.5 Estimation of the demand system	44
PART II: EMPIRICAL ANALYSIS OF STABILIZATION POLICIES	50-63
CHAPTER IV: EMPIRICAL EFFECTS OF BUDGETARY/DEVALUATION WAGE POLICIES AND EXTERNAL SHOCKS	50-63
4.1 Empirical effects of budgetary policies	50
4.2 Empirical effects of devaluation	57
4.3 Empirical effects of wage policies	61
4.4 External shocks	61
CHAPTER V: DIFFERENT MIXTURES WITHIN POLICY PACKAGES	64-67
5.1 The traditional stabilization package	64
5.2 An outward-oriented package	66
5.3 Trade-offs and constraints	67

TABLE OF CONTENTS (cont'd)

	Pages
PART III: EMPIRICAL ANALYSIS OF STRUCTURAL ADJUSTMENT POLICIES	68-82
CHAPTER VI: EMPIRICAL EFFECTS OF STRUCTURAL ADJUSTMENT POLICIES	68-76
6.1 Trade liberalization	68
6.2 Tax reform	73
6.3 Other supply-side policies: agricultural sector adjustment	74
CHAPTER VII: STABILIZATION-CUM-STRUCTURAL ADJUSTMENT POLICIES	77-82
7.1 Fine-tuning of stabilization-cum-structural adjustment	77
7.2 Social costs of stabilization and adjustment	79
7.3 Conclusions and limitations of results of the models	81
ANNEX I: THE PHOSPHATE SECTOR AND MARKET	83-88
ANNEX II:	89-117
A. Mathematical structure of the model	89
B. Sector specification	103
C. Supply and demand elasticities in the model	116

PART I: THE GENERAL EQUILIBRIUM MODEL OF MOROCCO STRUCTURE, DATA AND MODEL SOLUTION

INTRODUCTION

1.   Like so many developing countries, Morocco has been experiencing an external debt crisis since 1983. The massive external debt build up resulting from the expansion of government expenditures after the floundering of the phosphate price boom and encouraged by the easy availability of international banking credit in the late 1970s and early 1980s has brought to the fore the structural problems of the economy. Besides the macro desequilibria originating in the large public deficit and exchange rate overvaluation, the inefficiency of productive factors has been one of the main preoccupations of the policy makers, particularly in view of the low growth experienced by the economy in the last five years. Despite the role played by the oil price shock and the debt shock of the early 80s, partly reversed in recent years, it is now widely recognized that domestic policies had a major responsability in the creation of those desequilibria. As most of the developing countries, Morocco had pursued during the 1960s and 1970s a development strategy based on high protection barriers and overvalued exchange rate, with State investment playing a dominant role.

2.   In order to place the economy onto a new sustainable growth path, a combination of stabilization and structural adjustment policies have been applied since 1983. They have already produced significant results. The current account has swung from an 8% deficit in 1982 to a 3% surplus, when interest payments are excluded. However, some structural problems related to factor efficiency and tax reform still remain. In fact, most of the adjustment has been achieved at the cost of drastically reducing public investment, which compromises future growth. The conflict between trade liberalization and fiscal policy still remains a major concern.

3.   The framework designed in this paper addresses some of these issues. In the context of stabilization, the policies of a reduction in government current and investment expenditures, an increase in taxes, and a devaluation are analyzed. Policy packages which contrast inward-oriented and outward-oriented are tested. The structural adjustment, or supply side, policies are addressed, including trade liberalization, tax reform, and agriculture price policies. Since we are only studying the real effects of those policies, the impact on aggregate and sectoral output, relative prices, external balance and budget are traced. Besides those impacts, the effect of policies on resource allocation is at the center of our concerns.

4.   The major conclusions of our analysis are: (i) a devaluation policy is less contractionary, in terms of output and employment, than a fiscal policy for a quick impact on the current account deficit; (ii) contraction of government investment is more effective in reducing external deficit, and decreases output and employment less than contraction of government consumption; (iii) an inward-oriented stabilization package based on fiscal contraction plus increase in protection is more contractionary than an outward-oriented package based on the same fiscal restraint and devaluation; (iv) the best growth enhancing strategy combines fiscal restraint with trade

liberalization and a compensatory devaluation; (v) tax reform that increases budget revenues and reduces distortions combined with incentives to private investment and public investment increase can also produce significant improvement in the efficiency of resources and on output; and finally (vi) several supply side policies characterized by sector adjustment policies that reduce distortions and improve production incentives can also produce significant output effects.

5.   After a period of steady growth under an import-substitution strategy in the 1965-73 period, Morocco experienced a "phosphate price boom" in 1974-76. The price of phosphate rock, its major exports (about one third of receipts), more than tripled. Although short lived, the boom touched off a large expansion of central government and public enterprise investment, sometimes of doubtful productivity, as well as expansion of social and other infrastructure recurrent expenditures. The war in the Sahara also led to a large expansion of military expenditures. Downward rigidity in most of these expenditures, low external real interest rates and abundance of external credit as well as sustained high expectations of a price recovery of phosphates led to a large build-up of external debt. The external crisis flared up in 1983 when the adverse effects of the 1979-83 external shocks hit the economy. Terms of trade deterioration, recession in external markets, increasing protectionism, and the sharp increase in world real interest rates amounted to an import equivalent to about 10 percent of GDP. In 1985 with an external debt of about $12 billion, three times the export revenues, and a debt service ratio of 70 percent before rescheduling, Morocco was one of the highest indebted countries in the world, and had to enter into a succession of debt reschedulings with its creditors.

6.   Since 1983 Morocco has embarked in a stabilization program to redress the domestic imbalances and regain creditworthiness. Policy makers realized that only a substantial structural adjustment in the economy could create the conditions for a sustained growth. Trade liberalization and export promotion were viewed as the best way to maintain growth short of a massive retrenchement of aggregate demand. Fiscal reform coupled with close scrutiny of government expenditures and global credit control could redress the budget deficit. Agricultural sector reforms would promote efficiency of resource use in irrigated areas and lead to expansion of productions where Morocco has comparative advantage.

7.   The framework used here to answer some of the policy questions raised by the need to reduce the macro-desequilibria and distortions is a computable general equilibrium model. The model draws on the general equilibrium theory and incorporates the main institutional characteristics of the Moroccan economy. As any policy model, it had to be focussed on certain policy questions. In terms of stabilization policies, it contains all the main instruments of fiscal and budgetary policies as well as control of the exchange rate. It is purely a real model. Monetary and financial mechanisms are not modeled.[1] The sectoral detail and the specification of production and demand functions by product allow the analysis of structural adjustment policies. Among others, this study analyzes trade liberalization, fiscal reform, and agricultural sector policies. Finally, the decomposition of

---

[1] For an analysis of the monetary mechanism, see A. Mateus, "A Macro-econometric Model for Stabilization Policies: the Case of Morocco", 1986.

households by income group and socio-economic groups allows the analysis of the social costs of adjustment of different policy paths.

8. The model is in the tradition of computable general equilibrium models initiated by J. Shoven and J. Whalley[1] that simulate a Walrasian economy. In these models, profit and utility maximization are specified as well as the essential properties of general equilibrium in terms of market adjustment. Price adjustment plays a major role. For the analysis of developing countries, the path-breaking work was done by Adelman and Robinson and Dervis, de Melo and Robinson.[2]

9. The main innovation of our model is the incorporation of the Scandinavian type of features in a general equilibrium model. The economy is divided into tradable and nontradable or quota protected sectors. In the latter, we assume a mark-up type of price-formulation consistent with most of the observations about oligopolistic markets. The other contribution is the need to interpret trade liberalization not only as reducing quantitative restrictions and tariffs but also as a change in market structures. Thus, the previous approach is transformed into a "neoclassical type" of model where the flex-price adjustment is the essential mechanism in the tradable sectors.

10. Plan of Work. Chapter I gives the background about the Moroccan economy. After an analysis of its structure, it brings forward the main characteristics of the policy problems affecting the economy and the recent programs of stabilization and adjustment undertaken. Chapter II explains the structure of the core model and the rationale of its sectoral specification. The mathematical specification is left to Annexes 2, and its computer program to Annex 3. Chapter III explains the construction of the data base and calibration of the model. Evidence is gathered to justify the parametrization of those functions and the method of calibration of the model is explained. The chapter closes with a brief analysis of the phosphate sector, which is central to the Moroccan economy.

11. The second part studies the use of the model in different policy areas. Chapter V studies the use of budgetary, devaluation and wages (incomes) policies as well as the impact of external shocks on the economy. Chapter VI combines some of these instruments in stabilization packages. An outward-oriented package relying on export promotion is contrasted with the more traditionally used import restraint package. The next chapter studies questions related with structural adjustment policies. In particular, three types of programs that have been at the center of the policy dialogue are analyzed: trade liberalization, fiscal reform and agricultural sector reforms. A closing chapter studies problems of fine-tuning stabilization and structural adjustment policies and the social costs of adjustment in terms of incidence of those programs by income group.

---

[1] See, H. Scarf and J. Shoven, Applied General Equilibrium Analysis, Cambridge University Press, 1984 for a recent survey of those models.

[2] I. Adelman and S. Robinson, Income Distribution Policies in Developing Countries, Stanford U. Press, 1978 and K. Dervis, J. de Melo and S. Robinson, General Equilibrium Models for Development Policy, Cambridge U. Press, 1982.

CHAPTER I

BACKGROUND

1. With a GNP of US$ 670 per capita in 1984, Morocco is slightly below the average of the lower middle-income countries. GNP grew at about 5.1% per year and population at 2.5% p.a. in the last two decades, comparable to that group of countries. Its population in mid-1984 was 21.4 million. A relatively open economy in terms of its share of external trade on GDP, it has still about 39.2% of the labor force working in agriculture (but almost half of the population dependent on its activity) generating 17% of domestic output. The economy is still largely dependent on phosphates (about 46.5% of exports in 1984). Morocco has the largest known reserves in the world of phosphate rock. Agricultural output is subject to large fluctuations due to the irregularity of rainfall, although the irrigated area has increased substantially. The economy is still characterized by a dualistic system: a large subsistence agriculture sector coexisting with modern farms and a large urban informal sector co-existing with modern industries and services.

1.1. Growth performance and supply side

2. After growing at a pace above the lower middle-income countries in the 1960s and until 1977, Morocco registered a GDP growth rate (Table 1.1) below those countries in the 1977-84 period (3.0 versus 4.1% p.a.).

3. The rate of investment increased from around 12% in the 1960s to a peak of 34.2% in 1977, fueled by revenues from the phosphate price boom. However, it could not be sustained for a long period due to the fact that the rate of domestic savings dropped dramatically from 19% in the early 1970s to 7-8% in the early 1980s. This drop can be largely attributed to the loss in the terms of trade, large negative public savings, and other expansionary policies. As capital inflows dried out, the rate of investment had to be adjusted downwards, reaching 21.1% in 1987. The incremental capital output ratio rose from a level of 3.0 in the 1960s to 4.2 in the 1970s and to 7-8 in the 1980s, reflecting a dramatic decline in the efficiency of investment, due to the fact that the economic structure was not able to produce enough tradables in the presence of the debt crisis, and to poor agricultural harvests.

4. The development strategy in the last two decades was based on heavy investment in irrigation in agriculture, the development of "forward-linkages" in the phosphate sector, and the build-up of material infrastructure. For most of the social indicators, Morocco trails the average for lower-middle income countries.

5. By sectors of activity, the sector with highest growth has been the Government (11.2% p.a. in the last decade), followed by construction (5.6% p.a.) and the industrial sector (4% p.a.). When adjusted for relative prices, the mining sector has also a high growth rate (6.0% p.a.). Agriculture has

suffered the most disappointing growth as a result of a succession of droughts and sectoral policies pursued during that period (0.6% p.a.). As a consequence of policies pursued by the Government, the sector of non-tradables (services, government plus construction) had the largest increase in the 1970s and early 1980s, among activity sectors.

Table 1.1: MOROCCO - GROSS DOMESTIC PRODUCT BY SECTOR, 1973-84

	Annual Growth Rate (%) (at constant prices)				Share of GDP (%) (at current prices)			
	1965-73	1973-77	1977-80	1980-84	1965	1973	1977	1984
Agriculture	2.6	-0.8	7.2	-2.6	20.1	20.8	16.4	16.6
Mining, Energy, Pub. Utilities	4.0	2.4	6.3	3.2	8.3	6.9	6.6	8.7
Manufacturing	6.9	6.1	3.9	1.0	16.7	17.3	16.6	16.4
Construction	13.9	27.2	-11.0	0.8	3.8	3.7	9.4	6.5
Services	7.2	7.8	1.8	2.2	40.9	41.6	39.7	39.3
Government	7.3	14.4	10.7	8.6	10.2	9.6	11.4	12.5
Gross Domestic Product	6.4	7.5	3.6	2.5	100.0	100.0	100.0	100.0

Source: Government of Morocco and World Bank estimates.

6. The structure of production has thus changed significantly during the last two decades. Agriculture production saw its share decrease from 20.1% to 16.6%, at the same time that construction increased its share from 3.8% to 6.5%, while the government's share increased from 10.2% to 12.5%. The most dynamic subsectors in terms of production were the phosphate sector, including derivatives, government, construction, cement, and irrigated agriculture.

7. With a population growth rate of 2.6% p.a. in the last decade, labor force has grown at about 3.2% p.a. due to the large share of youth entering into the labor market. Employment in agriculture has expanded at less than 1% per year, while industry and services have created most of the employment (6-7% p.a.). The growth of labor productivity has so far been disappointing. In the last decade, it grew merely 1.4% per year. It fell in agriculture by 1.2% p.a., and increased in manufacturing by only 0.7% p.a. The lack of a more dynamic growth of output has thus caused unemployment (about 11%) and underemployment (estimated at between 30 and 40%) to remain high. At the same time, employment creation has been less than expected, due to the capital intensity of new investment (phosphate derivatives, heavy irrigation, sugar, etc.).

1.2. Demand management

8.   The expansionary policies (Table 1.2) which dominated the Moroccan economic scene in the 1970s were initially triggered by the sudden quadrupling of phosphate prices which accompanied the commodity price boom of the mid-1970s, greatly inflating Morocco's export earnings and fiscal revenues. In response to this windfall, the Government tripled the investment program, increased substantially government wages and vastly expanded its activities in the social sectors. It also initiated a major defense build-up to deal with the Sahara problem. The phosphate boom was short-lived, however, and the rigidities in the budgetary system led the Government to increase substantially its deficit. Coupled with the second oil shock, this led to large fiscal and external payments imbalances and rapid growth of the external debt (Graph 1), helped by the easy terms of foreign credit.

9.   Fiscal policy was largely expansionary from 1975 until 1982 (with a temporary contraction in 1978). The Public Administration deficit jumped from 4.8% of GDP in 1973 to 19.3% in 1976, and in 1982 was still 15.2% (Graph 3). The structural deficit, adjusting for inflation and cyclical factors, reached an all-time high of 11.5% of GDP in 1977 and remained at 8% for most of the 1980s. With debt relief, it has dropped recently to 5%, but without further debt relief, it still remains at about 11%. Government revenue has increased only 5 percentage points of GDP in the last decade and a half, while current expenditures jumped about 7 points. Capital expenditures have experienced large swings: they increased from 8% of GDP in 1973 to 16.6% in 1977. They were reduced slightly to 13% in 1983. In the last years they have been drastically reduced to 3.5% of GDP in 1987. The increase in recurrent expenditures was in terms of expansion in public employment, interest payments and food subsidies. State investment was heavily oriented towards irrigation, education and infrastructures. However, some of the projects have been shown to have a doubtful return [1]/ or a long gestation period. On the other side, the large public enterprise system has invested heavily on the phosphate sector, energy, and some industrial subsectors. The latter have also shown sometimes low rates of return.

10.   The Government deficit has been largely financed by recourse to external financing (about two thirds). Use of foreign savings has averaged about 6% of GDP in the 1980-85 period. However, since the late 1970s, domestic credit has expanded much more rapidly than money, the rate of intermediation has stagnated, and additional domestic resources have been mobilized to cover the public sector deficit. Seignorage has also been financing the deficit in the equivalent of about 4% of GDP. The build-up of large arrears in payments by the Treasury has been one of the major sources of financing the deficit. This has caused a recessionary impact on domestic activity but had the benefit of maintaining a low inflation rate. The external debt build-up has put Morocco in the group of heavily-indebted countries. Debt-service ratio (based on exports of goods and services) increased from 7.2% in 1975 to 49.0% in 1982, and reached 68% in 1986, before debt relief. The stock of the external debt over exports increased from 78%

---

[1]/ See World Bank Report, Morocco - Priorities for Public Sector Investment (1981-85), June 1983.

in 1975 to 310% in recent years (Graph 1). The probability of occurrence of a major debt crisis crossed the critical level in 1979 and reached almost .9 in 1982. In fact, in 1983, Morocco had to reschedule its private and official external debt. Although the real exchange rate, using the CPI as deflator (Graph 3), remained constant in 1973-79, using the WPI indicates it appreciated by about 12%. The steep increase in effective protection due to the increase of the "taxe spéciale" and the extensive use of QR's for all imported goods that had import substitutes meant that the exchange rate was already largely overvalued by 1980. From 1980 to 1983, the dirham had a real devaluation of almost 14% (the terms of trade decreased by about 8%) but its effect on the balance of payments was largely nullified by the high rate of domestic absorption caused by the monetary and fiscal policies. In the 1983-86 period, Morocco depreciated the real effective exchange rate by 12%, an important factor in the adjustment process.

11. The current account deficit, which had reached an all time high in 1977 (16.5% of GDP), declined until 1980. However, the conjugation of the external shock (terms of trade deterioration, recession in industrialized countries, increased protectionism, and increased real world interest rates) with the overvaluation of the exchange rate and the new expansionary investment program of 1982 led to a new deterioration in 1981/82 to 12.6% of GDP.

12. Morocco had certainly not experienced the phenomenal increase in exports of manufactures of the NICs. In fact, the poor performance of Morocco's exports is clearly demonstrated by the evolution of its share in developed country imports which decreased from 2.2% in 1970 to 1.6% in 1980. From 1980 to 1985 the share appears to have remained constant. Agricultural exports have performed particularly poorly over the past 15 years, which led to a sharp decline in their share of total exports from 55% in the early seventies to about 25% in recent years. Phosphate exports, on the other hand, have increased their share in total export earnings to nearly 50% (including phosphoric acid and fertilizers) and new additions to processing capacity currently under construction are likely to further accentuate Morocco's dependence on the volatile world market for phosphate fertilizers over the next few years. This unbalanced trade pattern has left Morocco in a highly vulnerable position for a prolonged period. Despite their relatively rapid growth in recent years, exports of manufactures (excluding foodstuffs and phosphate products) still account only for 20% of total merchandise exports. It is only in textiles, footwear, and clothing that Morocco has gained a substantial increase in developed country imports (its share has increased three times in the first two and eight times in the third product, during the 1970-83 period). Morocco has been displacing most of the South European countries in the supply of nonskilled labor intensive goods to Europe.

1.3. The 1983-85 Adjustment cum-Structural Adjustment Program

13. Starting from a low-debt position in 1974, Morocco was by the mid 1980s one of the most highly indebted countries in the world (total debt over GDP exceeds 110%, and debt service over exports has been above 55% in the last three years before rescheduling). This debt build-up can be largely ascribed to the government deficit. In 1983, Morocco's access to international financial markets was sharply reduced, and expectations of further increases

Table 1.2: MAIN MACROECONOMIC INDICATORS

	Average 1965-72	1973	1975	1977	Average 1973-78	1979	1980	1981	1982	1983	1984	Average 1979-84	1985	1986	1987[E]
Exports of Goods & NFS	659.7	1287.5	1997.3	1838.8	1843.6	2706.8	3272.6	3082.0	2968.9	2993.8	3037.9	2990.4	3184.9	3605.7	4156.8
Imports of Goods & NFS	713.2	1356.5	2952.8	4061.8	2984.9	4751.9	5247.5	5310.2	5198.5	4223.0	4389.8	4809.7	4341.3	4468.4	4879.4
Current Account Deficit	-78.2	-63.2	-562.2	-1870.4	-828.5	-1530.4	-1420.7	-1861.8	-1898.4	-1000.2	-1205.3	-1571.9	-880.5	-226.9	-74.2
% GDP	-1.8	-1.7	-6.1	-16.5	-7.1	-9.6	-8.0	-12.5	-12.7	-7.5	-10.1	-10.1	-7.4	-1.5	-0.4
Total External Debt[1]	919.1	997.8	1752.5	4069.4	5123.2	6182.0	9589.0	1102.1	1241.9	1382.9	1407.4	1218.6	1714.6	1927.9	1829.5
Rate of Investment	15.3	16.9	25.2	34.2	25.1	24.5	22.6	22.4	23.3	20.9	21.7	22.6	21.9	23.2	21.1
Rate of Domestic Savings	13.5	18.6	19.1	13.8	16.3	11.6	11.5	7.4	8.4	11.6	10.4	10.2	12.2	17.4	16.8
Exports of gnfs/GDP	18	20	23	16.9	20.5	17.0	18.4	20.8	19.8	22.5	25.5	20.7	26.8	24.4	24.9
Imports of gnfs/GDP	20	22	33	37.3	31.4	29.9	29.4	35.8	34.8	31.7	36.9	32.1	36.5	30.2	29.2
GDP growth rate	5.1	3.6	7.6	6.1	6.0	4.8	3.6	-1.3	5.6	3.4	1.5	3.2	2.9	6.4	1.8
Inflation	1.5	4.0	8.0	12.5	10.9	8.4	9.4	12.5	10.5	6.2	12.5	9.4	7.7	8.8	4.5
Money GDP	28	33	36	36	35	38	36	38	36	35.9	35.9	37.2	35.1	36.1	35.7
Domestic Credit/GDP	28	31	35	38	36	43	43	46	42	53.6	53.0	45.5	53.6	51.5	50.0
Government Revenue/GDP	19	19.9	26.8	24.7	23.9	24.3	26.1	28.4	26.8	26.2	25.8	26.3	24.8	24.6	23.8
Current Exp./GDP	17	16.6	29.8	25.6	25.2	26.6	28.8	31.2	29.1	30.1	30.0	29.3	28.7	26.5	25.5
Capital Exp./GDP	5	8.1	11.8	16.6	11.2	9.0	7.4	10.0	12.9	8.2	8.3	9.3	6.2	4.1	3.5
Structural deficit estimates		-0.4	-12.8	-11.5	-3.9	-5.1	-5.6	-8.3	-8.3	-8.0	-8.7	-5.7	-7.3	-4.6	-4.9

1/ Medium and long-term official debt until 1979.

Source: IMF, IFS and National Accounts.

November 1987

Graph 1
RATIO EXTERNAL DEBT OVER EXPORTS
DOD MLT Over Exp. goods and nfs and wr

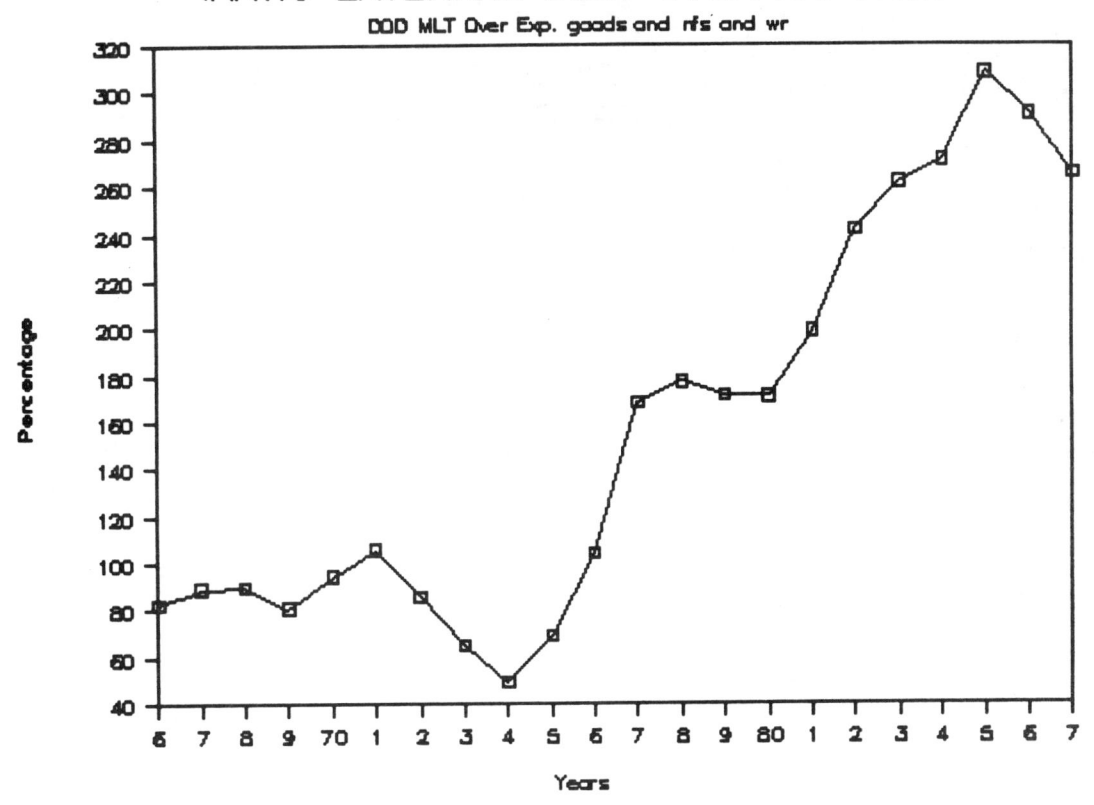

Graph 2
DEBT SERVICE RATIO
Over Exp. Goods&Services, before resch.

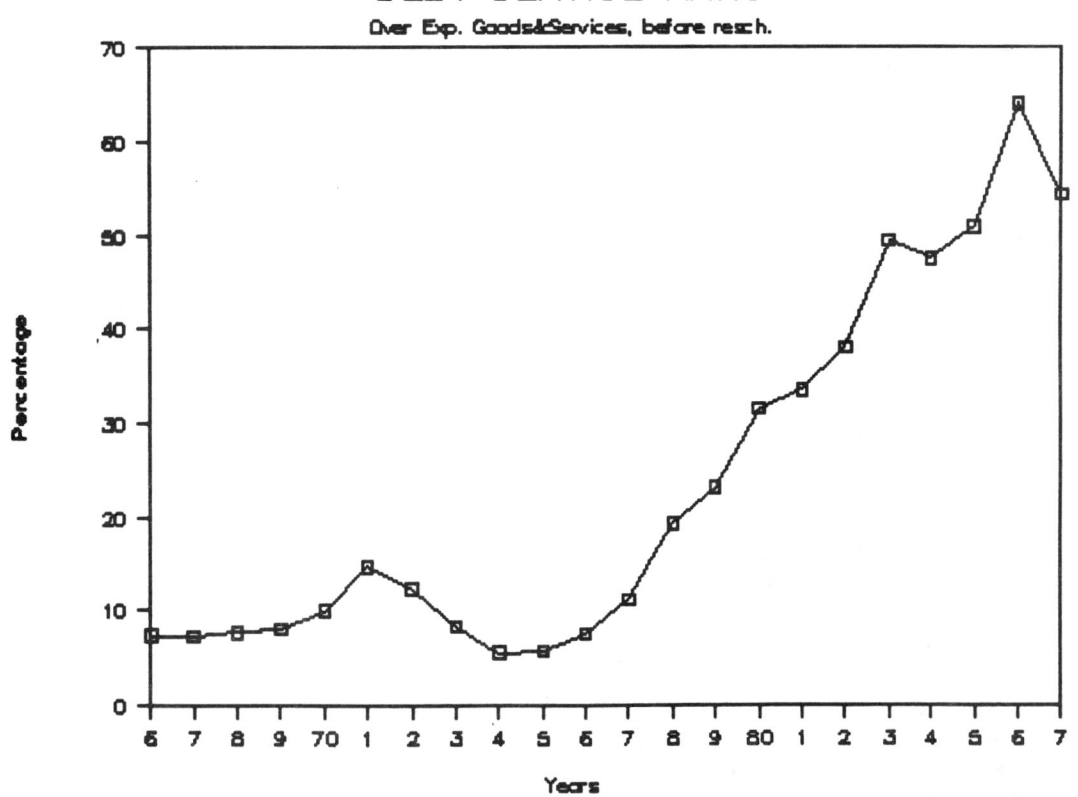

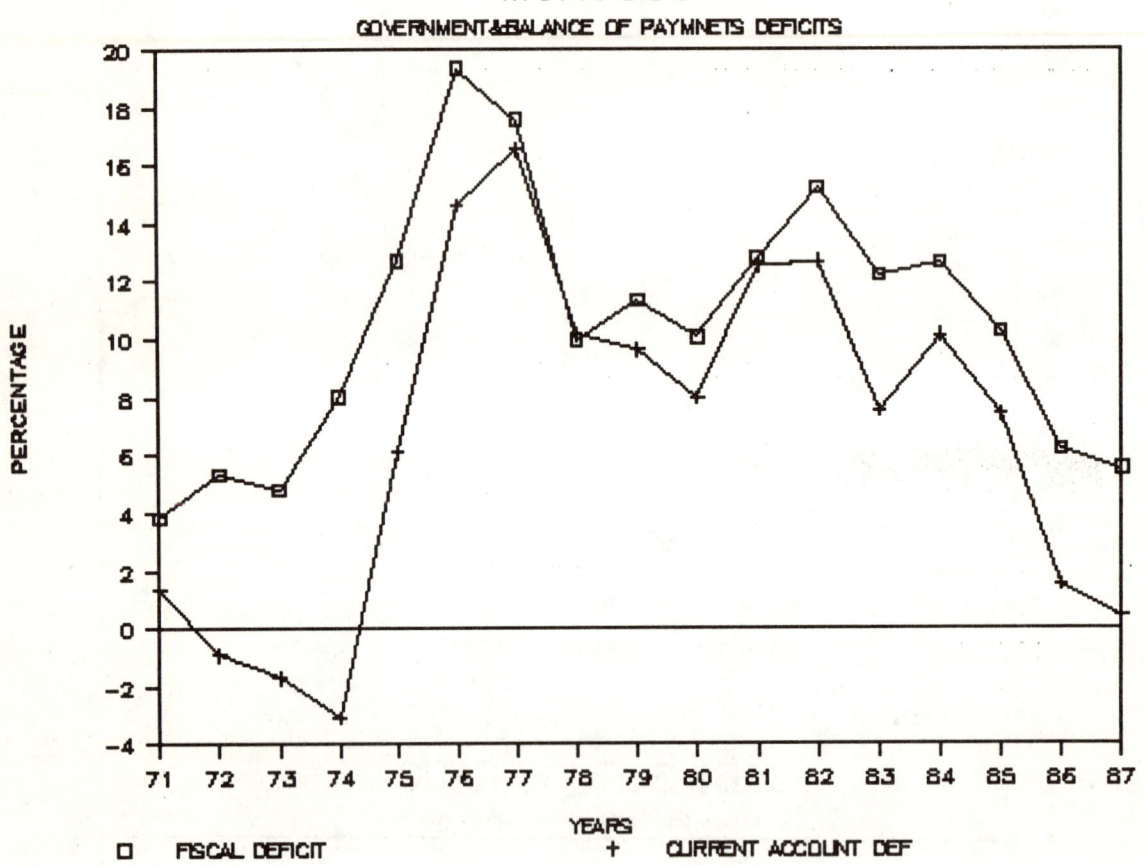

Graph 3
MOROCCO
GOVERNMENT&BALANCE OF PAYMNETS DEFICITS

□ FISCAL DEFICIT   + CURRENT ACCOUNT DEF

in flows of concessional assistance failed to materialize. Foreign exchange reserves, already very low, virtually disappeared, prompting the Government to impose emergency import restrictions in March. The level of new budgetary investment appropriations had to be curtailed. Concurrently, a new stabilization program was prepared and supported by an 18-month IMF stand-by arrangement. The principal objective of the stand-by (which covered the July 1983 - December 1984 period) was to reduce the current account deficit of the balance of payments before debt relief from 13% of GDP in 1982 to 9% in 1983 and to a target of 7.3% by 1984 through limits on monetary expansion, reductions in the Government deficit, and continued use of a flexible exchange rate policy. The program envisaged a reduction in the Government budget deficit (before relief on interest payments from debt rescheduling) from more than 12% of GDP in 1982 to 8.7% in 1983 and a target of 7.8% in 1984 on a cash basis. To contain the deficit from what was originally approved, the Government raised the price of subsidized foodstuffs, increased the price of fertilizers, electricity, water, and petroleum products, reduced net public service recruitment, and reduced capital appropriations. The same measures were pursued in 1984.

14. Along with this stabilization effort, Morocco also made a start on the structural reforms needed to restore a viable balance-of-payments position in the medium term with a package of measures to restructure trade incentives in order to eliminate the bias in favor of production for the domestic market as compared with exports and to promote the efficient use of resources. In January 1984, the Bank approved an Industrial and Trade Policy Adjustment loan (ITPA I) [1]/ to support the first phase of this program.

15. The profitability of production for export was substantially increased as a result of a depreciation of the real effective exchange rate. At the same time, imports were liberalized; the special import tax was reduced from 15 to 10%; the remaining prior import deposit requirements were reduced from 15 to 10% in January 1984 and eliminated in July; and the maximum rate of customs duty was reduced to 60% so as to decrease the excessively high incentives previously granted to some import-substituting industries. In addition, the emergency quantitative import restrictions that had been imposed in March 1983 were progressively removed.

16. On the export side, special customs regimes for exporters were extended and improved; export licensing was removed for all but a few products; and the monopoly of the state marketing board (OCE) on exports of processed food products was abolished. In parallel to these external trade measures, the Government also implemented in 1983 and 1984 a reform of the system of export credit and export credit insurance and a substantial increase in interest rates on remittances of overseas workers. In addition, the first phase of a major program of liberalization of domestic price controls in the manufacturing sector was carried out.

17. The results suggest that the policies adopted since 1983 have had a positive impact. In 1983, the resource gap was substantially reduced, from about 15% of GDP in 1982 to 9%. This was achieved through a significant

___

1/ For details on this program, see World Bank Report No. P-3707-MOR.

decline in the GDP share of consumption, investment and imports relative to their high levels in recent years. The share of exports and gross domestic savings increased substantially. The current account deficit of the balance of payments (before debt relief) was reduced from $1.9 billion or 12.7% of GDP in 1982 to $1.0 billion or 7.5% of GDP in 1983, overshooting by 1 percentage point the IMF stand-by target. The Government budget deficit, largely financed by the build-up of arrears, was reduced from 15.2% in 1982 to 12.1% of GDP in 1983.

18.   In 1984 the pace of adjustment slowed significantly, owing both to unfavorable weather conditions and to the fact that the better-than-expected balance-of-payments results achieved in 1983 had stemmed, in part, from exceptional factors. The current account deficit of the balance of payments levelled off in 1984 at about $1.2 billion (10% of GDP), but represented an increase of 1.8 percentage points over the IMF stand-by target for 1984. There was continued favorable response of manufactured exports (other than food and phosphate) and tourism receipts, and their share of GDP increased about 6 percentage points relative to 1982, while imports maintained their share. The budget deficit maintained the same share of GDP (12.5%), if arrears are taken into account far from the IMF target.

19.   In 1985 the Government continued its efforts of trade liberalization and export promotion supported by a second Industrial and Trade Policy Adjustment loan from the World Bank. A key instrument to achieve the objectives was a 8-9% real devaluation that maintained the competitivity of Moroccan exports and compensated, on the import side, for the progressive decline in protection that resulted from trade liberalization. The special import tax, which was reduced from 15 to 10% in January 1984 was further cut to 7.5% in January 1985. The SIT was expected to be eliminated by January 1987. In addition, in order to reverse the costly import substitution process which occurred in the past as a result of high protection levels, the maximum rate of customs duties, which was reduced to 60% in 1984, was lowered to 45% in 1985, equivalent to about 60% of nominal protection. The medium-term objective in tariff policy was to reduce the overall level of protection to 25% through decreasing maximum duty rates and evening out the spread in tariff rates within and between sectors.

20.   During 1985, GDP growth picked-up strength due to a better than normal agricultural year, after having been sluggish in the previous two years. The current account deficit (before debt relief) improved 1.7 percentage points to 7.4% of GDP. However, both the government deficit and the credit to the economy failed to meet the targets under the stand-by program with the IMF. The government deficit, including arrears, improved only marginally to reach about 10.1% of GDP.

21.   The drop in international prices of oil and wheat in 1986 accompanied by a record crop had a major favorable effect in the balance of payments, equivalent to 4% of GDP. Unable to resolve differences, the existing stand-by was declared inoperative. A new stand-by was approved in November 1986 supporting a program of: (a) reducing the external current account deficit from 1.7% of GDP in 1986 to zero in 1987 with the elimination of external

arrears and increases in foreign exchange reserves to the equivalent of one month of imports; (b) reducing the fiscal deficit, on a payment order basis, from 6.6% of GDP in 1986 to 4.3% in 1987; (c) holding the rate of increase of domestic bank credit at 7.1% in 1987. According to preliminary estimates, these targets may be fulfilled in regards to the external and Treasury deficits. Although the situation has not improved in terms of foreign exchange flows. There was also a retrenchment both of imports and exports in terms of GDP. In fact, most of the improvement in the external current account came from a reduction of about 7 percentage points of GDP in imports due to lower expenditures on oil and wheat. Similarly, a large part of the improvement in the fiscal deficit resulted from a reduction in capital expenditures of 6 percentage points of GDP relative to the 1979-84 average.

22. Since 1983, Morocco has been benefitting from debt relief. The London Club has been rescheduling all commercial debt principal, and the Paris Club has rescheduled principal and part of interest. Overall, debt relief has been provided in the amount of 1.2 to 1.5 billion dollars per year in terms of amortization. It was only after the favorable shock of 1986 that current account, excluding interest payments, started to generate a surplus of about 3.5% of GDP, which represents a significant step towards creditworthiness.

1.4. Incentives policies

23. The Government has intervened extensively in economic activity by using <u>differential commodity taxation</u>, tariffs and subsidies, <u>producer and investment subsidies</u> to give incentives to production in special targeted sectors; wide use of <u>quantitative restrictions</u> on imports that compete with domestic production or basic staples; and <u>price intervention</u> for some basic goods (foodstuffs, energy, fertilizers, etc.). This system of incentives has largely distorted market prices, rates of return and, due to the wide range of sometimes conflicting economic objectives pursued, has defeated its main purposes.

24. A study of the <u>protection system</u> of the industrial sector (see Morocco: Industrial Incentives and Export Promotion, World Bank, 1983, specially the Annex on Protection, pages 172-190) showed that for most of the industrial products produced domestically, nominal custom duties cluster around 50 to 100%. Since most of the industrial inputs have lower rates of duties, rates of effective protection were often very high. Even more important, the administration has mounted since the 1960s a pervasive system of quantitative restrictions (mainly quotas) that has pursued the double objective of generally restricting the level of imports in years of balance of payments crisis and of protecting the domestic industrial structure. It is widely believed that the levels of protection reached an all time high in 1983. In the traded products of the agriculture sector, except for sugar, the rate of effective protection is lower than industry. Most of the time, cereals (the largest agricultural output) have had a largely negative rate of effective protection. Also here, quantitative restrictions pervade the whole sector.

25.   Consumer subsidies have been used to stabilize prices, as an income transfer to the poor and to keep wages lower. However, they have been used mainly in imported goods, and their use in conjunction with price controls and quotas have led to adverse impact on domestic production. Before the middle of the 1970s, there was a scheme of price stabilization of consumer prices for basic foodstuffs (cereals, sugar, edible oils, milk, butter and petroleum products). However, after 1975, the Treasury had to start to allocate funds to finance that scheme when the government refused to increase prices enough to cover average costs. In the early 1980s, when those prices had to rise due to devaluation and the commodity price boom, the Government intervened and spent up to 10% of its recurrent expenditures in subsidizing food prices. The rates of subsidy in soft wheat flour and edible oils were about 50% of the import cost. Producer subsidies have been used largely in irrigation and sugar production, to stimulate the livestock subsector, in agricultural inputs, and for exports. Producer incentives have pursued the laudable objective of promoting certain types of production, but over the long-term, they distort market allocations. Investment subsidies have also been used for most of the sectors, especially in irrigated agriculture, manufacturing, construction, transport, and tourism. Although they had been devised to promote investment, they can be rationalized only as a temporary cyclical policy to promote recovery. Over the long-term, non-uniformity leads to wrong signals in terms of rates of returns and biases investment towards capital-intensive techniques and sectors.

26.   Finally, maintaining an overvalued exchange rate not only discouraged exports but also lead to over-capitalization of investments, deprotecting import substituting sectors and distorting prices of tradables versus non-tradables.

1.5. Sector Strategies

27.   Appropriate sector strategies were developed for the key productive sectors after 1983, particularly agriculture and industry, in order to increase productivity, encourage exports and efficient import substitution, and remove institutional and other obstacles to efficient resource use. In industry, although the development of Morocco's potential for export of phosphate fertilizers will continue to be an important objective, a high degree of dependence on phosphate and phosphate fertilizer exports has made Morocco extremely vulnerable to cyclical fluctuations in the volatile world phosphate market (para. 44). For this reason, the industrial strategy must be based on the promotion and diversification of manufactured exports, including processed foods and nontraditional manufactures where Morocco may have a comparative advantage on world markets.

28.   In agriculture, productivity is low and output has remained stagnant, except in irrigated areas at the cost of massive subsidies. In this sector, Morocco needs to develop a complex package of policies to overcome existing constraints to rational land use patterns. It will also be necessary to ensure that farmers have adequate incentives to improve farming techniques and use modern inputs, and to provide the support services needed to bring about these changes. Such a strategy calls for coordinated actions on a broad front, including changes in producer price and credit policies,

rationalization of input prices, strengthening of the research and extension system, improvements in marketing mechanisms, and in the availability of seeds and fertilizers. Progress has been made in some of these areas in recent years, but much remains to be done. The Bank is supporting reforms in a number of these areas through project lending and a recently-approved Agricultural Sector Policy Adjustment loan.[1]

1.6. Investment Policies

29. The low productivity of investment has been one of the major factors in the poor performance of the Moroccan economy in the past 10 years. The allocation of capital and the efficiency of investment need to be improved considerably both in the public and in the private sector. In the private sector, the reform of the protection framework described above should go a long way towards removing distortions in investment patterns. However, it would also be necessary to review the bias in favor of capital-intensive activities inherent in the current investment incentive system, including tax exemptions and interest rate subsidies which artificially depress the cost of capital. Pricing capital at its true opportunity cost would help correct the existing bias against labor-intensive activites which has hampered employment creation in the past and led to high investment costs per job in the industrial sector. More efficient use of capital would also be promoted by a program of financial sector reforms designed to improve financial intermediation. This program includes measures to promote deregulation, increased competition and adjustments in credit allocation and interest rate policies. A number of steps have been taken in this area in 1984, and further liberalization of lending rates as well as phasing out of credit rationing are expected to take place under ITPA II.[2]

30. In the public sector, to increase the efficiency of investment would require a considerable improvement of existing planning and budgeting mechanisms, including better procedures for setting investment priorities, strengthening of project preparation and monitoring capability, and placing more emphasis on the economic evaluation of projects before funds are allocated to them. In the immediate future, a solution must be found for the current high level of appropriations carry-over in the investment budget. Government efforts to review and reprogram the ongoing portfolio of investment projects in light of resource availabilities and relative priorities need to be continued. The weaning out of projects and activities with relatively low priority will not only help relieve pressure on scarce budgetary resources but also enable executing agencies to gain better control over the implementation schedules of higher priority investments, for which funding could be assured. In the medium-term, new planning and budgeting systems still need to be developed, along with adequate monitoring mechanisms for both Government and public enterprise investments.

---

[1] For details on the program of agricultural sector policy reforms, see Report No. P-4032-MOR.
[2] See Report No. P-4075-MOR for details.

1.7. External Trade Strategies and Openness of the Economy.

31.   <u>Import substitution</u>. During the 1958-69 period, Morocco pursued a policy of import substitution in most non-durable consumer goods, namely food, beverages and tobacco, textiles and clothing. It also achieved a reduction in the import ratio for some intermediate goods, like wood and furniture, paper and printing, rubber and plastics and some chemicals (Table 1.3). By the end of the 1960s, imports provided less than 11% of supply in the food industries, beverages and tobacco, clothing, leather and shoes, and cement. During the 1970s, the strategy for import substitution and the increased import controls, led to a decrease in the import ratio in almost all sectors and particularly in metallurgy and metalworking (from 80% in 1969 to 30% in 1980[1/]), textiles (from 25% to 14.1%) and chemicals (from 36% to 23%). By 1985, most of the import ratios increased, mainly due to some easing of the pervasive quantitative restriction system that reached its peak in 1983.

32.   The remaining potential for import substitution can be roughly assessed by comparing output multipliers using the total coefficients of the input-output matrix (i.e. including imports) with output multipliers excluding final and intermediate imports. The analysis reveals three broad categories of industries where further import substitution may be possible. The first group is machinery, metalworking, transport equipment, and electrical products,[2/] which have a large differential between total and domestic coefficients and are relatively labor intensive. In all these sectors economies of scale are extremely important and require engineering and qualified and semi-qualified labor. Thus, it is still early for Morocco to take full advantage of that dynamic comparative advantage. The second group are industries based on agricultural products, where the slackening of the growth of agricultural output has caused a large increase in imported inputs (food industries, in general). The third group is other natural resource based industries that by incorporating more domestic value added can reduce substantially the average import content of the sector (phosphate transformation, wood and furniture and paper and paper products).

33.   <u>Structure and Evolution of Exports</u>. After an initial period (1967-72) during which exports of goods and nonfactor services increased by 8.3% p.a. in volume, they rose only slightly by 1.2% p.a. from 1972 to 1980. This result was mainly due to the fall in exports of food and agricultural products, stagnation in tourism earnings, and slow growth in mining exports. However, there is ample evidence that the deceleration was associated with the "dutch disease" in the 1970s and the overvaluation of the dirham. It is only for phosphoric acid (production started in 1976) and for other related chemical products that exports expanded significantly.[3/] From 1980 to 1985, exports regained some dynamism, increasing at 4.5% p.a. largely due to the policies referred above.

1/ Production remains very small in this sector.
2/ These have been the object of a World Bank study "Morocco: The Engineering Industries", 1978.
3/ Exports of manufactured products (phosphoric acid, fertilizer and food products excluded) increased by 9.7% p.a. in 1969 prices from 1972 to 1980 and then accelerated to 12% in 1980/84.

Table 1.3: SHARES OF IMPORTS IN TOTAL SUPPLY
OF MANUFACTURED PRODUCTS

	Imports as a percentage of Imports plus Production					
	1958	1969	1975	1978	1980	1985
Food	18.4	18.8	16.0	8.3	9.8	10.5
Beverages and Tobacco	14.1	4.1	3.1	4.1	2.4	7.3
Textiles	39.0	25.2	18.6	18.1	14.1	17.1
Clothing	45.3	4.3	1.5	1.2	0.1	0.1
Leather and shoes	7.6	7.0	2.6	3.2	1.6	0.9
Wood and furniture	40.6	22.0	12.9	19.9	13.2	13.8
Paper and printing	36.8	20.8	24.2	21.0	20.2	19.0
Rubber and plastics	92.1	21.0	23.4	20.4	14.5	22.7
Chemicals	54.3	35.6	42.6	34.8	22.8	18.2
Non-metallic mineral products	12.7	11.2	16.3	20.4	7.1	8.2
Base metals and metalworking	64.0	79.9	45.9	40.7	29.5	37.2
Electrical and Machinery material	45.8	49.0	76.5	70.4	54.1	50.0
Transport equipment	54.5	44.8	53.6	51.7	32.3	46.3
Office machines, measure instruments, watches, etc.	–	–	48.5	46.7	49.0	57.9
Memo:						
Agricultural goods	6.2	7.4	17.9	10.8	7.5	8.0

Source: Input-output Tables

34. In the last two decades, exports diversified somewhat due to the growth of manufactured products (mainly textiles) and phosphate derivatives. The development of those exports seems to correspond to Morocco's comparative advantage, stemming from large phosphate reserves and the low cost of labor. On the other hand, the sharp reduction in the share of food and agricultural exports do not seem to match Morocco's comparative advantage, but seem largely associated with rising protectionism in the EEC in the last two decades, and domestic price policies.

35. In the first decade of Morocco's independence, about 60-70% of its exports were concentrated in phosphates and agricultural products. At the same time, the first steps were taken to increase exports of textiles, clothing, leather and shoes, and some food products. In 1984, manufactured exports represented about 42% and phosphate rock 24% of exports of goods. Within manufacturing, chemicals have already taken the largest share (52.8%)

due to the development of phosphoric acid and fertilizers, followed by textiles and clothing (26.6%). All the other manufactured exports represent only 14.2% of the total. The largest increase in share was for chemicals, textiles and clothing. The exports of fresh fish have also shown a large expansion.

36. **Export production shares.** In the 1969-80 period, there was a generalized drop in export orientation of Moroccan manufacturing, certainly associated with the discouraging effects on exports of the import subsitution strategy, overvaluation of the currency, and high protection rates. There were large decreases in the export shares in food industries (from 16% to 7%), clothing (from 12.5 to 9%), leather and shoes (from 23% to 12%), wood and furniture (15% to 2%), paper and printing (from 13% to 6%), basic metals and metalworking (from 22% to 4%) and transport equipment (from 6% to 4%), but these last two exports started with a very small level. In the first half of the 1980s, almost all the export/production ratios increased. Most significant was the increase in clothing and chemicals. Apart from chemicals, clothing, textiles and leather and shoes, external demand still plays a minor role in domestic output.

Table 1.4: PERCENTAGE OF MANUFACTURING PRODUCTION EXPORTED

	\multicolumn{6}{c}{Export/Production (%)}
	1958	1969	1975	1978	1980	1985
Food	11.8	16.1	6.7	6.4	6.6	8.0
Beverages and tobacco	1.3	11.4	4.4	1.8	1.6	1.8
Textiles	5.0	8.8	13.7	16.7	8.6	11.6
Clothing	7.9	12.5	17.8	23.4	9.4	22.4
Leather and footwear	12.6	23.0	20.8	17.7	11.8	12.5
Wood and furniture	33.5	15.1	5.6	6.1	2.4	2.7
Paper and printing	24.4	12.5	10.5	6.3	6.0	8.8
Rubber and plastics	0.0	1.9	4.4	1.1	0.7	3.0
Chemical products	19.8	14.6	12.3	22.8	14.7	30.5
Nonmetallic mineral products	8.2	2.7	2.2	1.0	0.6	1.0
Base metals and metal working	86.7	22.2	4.7	5.2	4.7	2.1
Electrical machinery and equipment	4.3	0.4	0.8	2.4	0.8	2.0
Transportation equipment	2.0	5.5	2.0	1.6	1.4	0.2
Office machines, measurement instruments, watches. etc.	-	-	8.7	18.8	0.5	0.4
Memorandum item: Agricultural products	20.3	21.3	11.8	9.9	7.3	7.8

Source: Input-output Tables.

CHAPTER II

THE BASIC GENERAL EQUILIBRIUM MODEL

2.1 An Overview of the Basic Model[1/]

37.   The core model of the Moroccan economy focuses on the distinction between tradables and nontradables sectors. In a typical tradables sector, exposed to international competition, the world price determines domestic price. In the classical formulation, with supply upward sloping and demand downward sloping, imports (or exports) are determined residually. Thus, an increase in prime costs (like raw materials and wages) would squeeze profits and decrease supply of tradables, and net exports would fall. A devaluation would have the opposite effect. In a typical nontradables sector domestic prices are isolated from world prices. Prices are based on prime costs using a mark-up adjustment, reflecting the profit calculation. In this case, supply is essentially elastic and the quantity produced is determined by demand.

38.   Since Morocco is a major exporter of phosphates, this sector has a dominant role in the economy (in terms of exports, government revenues, and all the other macroeconomic variables). Because exports are determined outside of the CGE in a model of the world market for phosphates with an oligopolistic structure, exports of this sector are taken exogenously.

39.   There are also important institutional constraints that should be taken into account in the formulation of a general equilibrium model for the Moroccan economy. First, in the short-run, agricultural production is mainly determined by weather conditions. Besides, most of the agricultural markets are isolated from world markets through quotas, tariffs, transport costs and differences in quality. In the case of cereals, the main agricultural product, international trade is forbidden, except for imports of soft wheat and maize which are controlled by a quota. There are also import monopolies for sugar and tea, and export monopolies for phosphates and agricultural products. The industrial sector is pervaded with protectionist policies. The effective rate of protection is estimated between 50 to 70%. Although the maximum basic tariff rate is now about 45%, there are still other custom duties that increase the duties paid by imports to about 55%. On the other hand, major exemptions of import duties apply to inputs used in exports and capital goods, and agricultural inputs. But the majority of the imports that compete with domestic production are still being controlled by quotas. Finally, another institutional aspect of the market adjustment that needs to be taken in consideration is price controls. In certain sectors like food industries, administered prices dominate the sector.

1/ See Annex II for the mathematical formulation.

40. The labor market is decomposed in formal and informal sectors. In the core model, wage rates are fixed in the formal sectors and labor supply is fixed in the informal market. Household consumption is determined by a system of demand functions decomposed by product and type of household.

41. Under the neoclassical "closure rule" capital stocks and total labor endowment are fixed and external savings exogenous. All prices are endogenous. However, our core static model uses a Keynesian type of "closure rule": investment is exogenous, domestic savings are endogenous and external savings are also endogenous. Nominal wages are fixed and consequently there is no assurance of full-employment. Since there is a large sector in the Moroccan economy outside of the fixed wage rule (informal plus family enterprises) the variation in labor income can be interpreted as a change in the return to sector specific factors and rents of those sectors.

42. The main focus of our model is on policy analysis: stabilization and structural adjustment policies. In the first case, government consumption and investment, devaluation and nominal wages are used to reach a certain objective of reduction in the external and public finance deficits. The second type of policies concentrate on fiscal reform, trade liberalization, and agricultural price polices. Fiscal reform is one of the areas frequently addressed by computable general equilibrium models. The question posed is how to change tax rates in order to increase tax revenues and improve efficiency in the economy. Trade liberalization problems address the macroeconomic impact of cutting the levels of protection in the economy. Finally, the general equilibrium model can be combined with a sector agricultural model in order to deal with the problem of elimination of input subsidies and output price support policies with the objective of increasing production.

2.2 The Supply Side and Production Structure

43. The general structure of the Moroccan general equilibrium model can be decomposed in a supply, a demand, and a price system (Diagram 1). We assume that there are two kinds of primary factors of production - capital and labor. There are 19 types of capital in the core model, specific to each sector of activity. Within each sector it can also be specific to the formal and informal subsectors. Labor is not homogeneous. It is disaggregated into 5 types, from non-skilled to technical and managerial labor. The aggregation is made with a two-level constant elasticity of substitution (CES) production function.

44. Imports come into the economy and pay all tariffs and other custom duties. Some goods, like petroleum, are assumed to have no domestic substitute in the short-term. For other goods like industrial food products, imports are assumed to be largely substitutable with domestic production. For most of the industrial and some of the agricultural goods, it is assumed that imports and domestic production have limited substitutability. This is the Armingtonian assumption that assumes a CES aggregation function. Its introduction tries to capture phenomena like the two-way trade in the same sector. The primary reason is that at the model level of aggregation, there are at the same time products that are imported and exported in the same

DIAGRAM 1

STRUCTURE OF THE GENERAL EQUILIBRIUM MODEL OF THE MOROCCAN ECONOMY

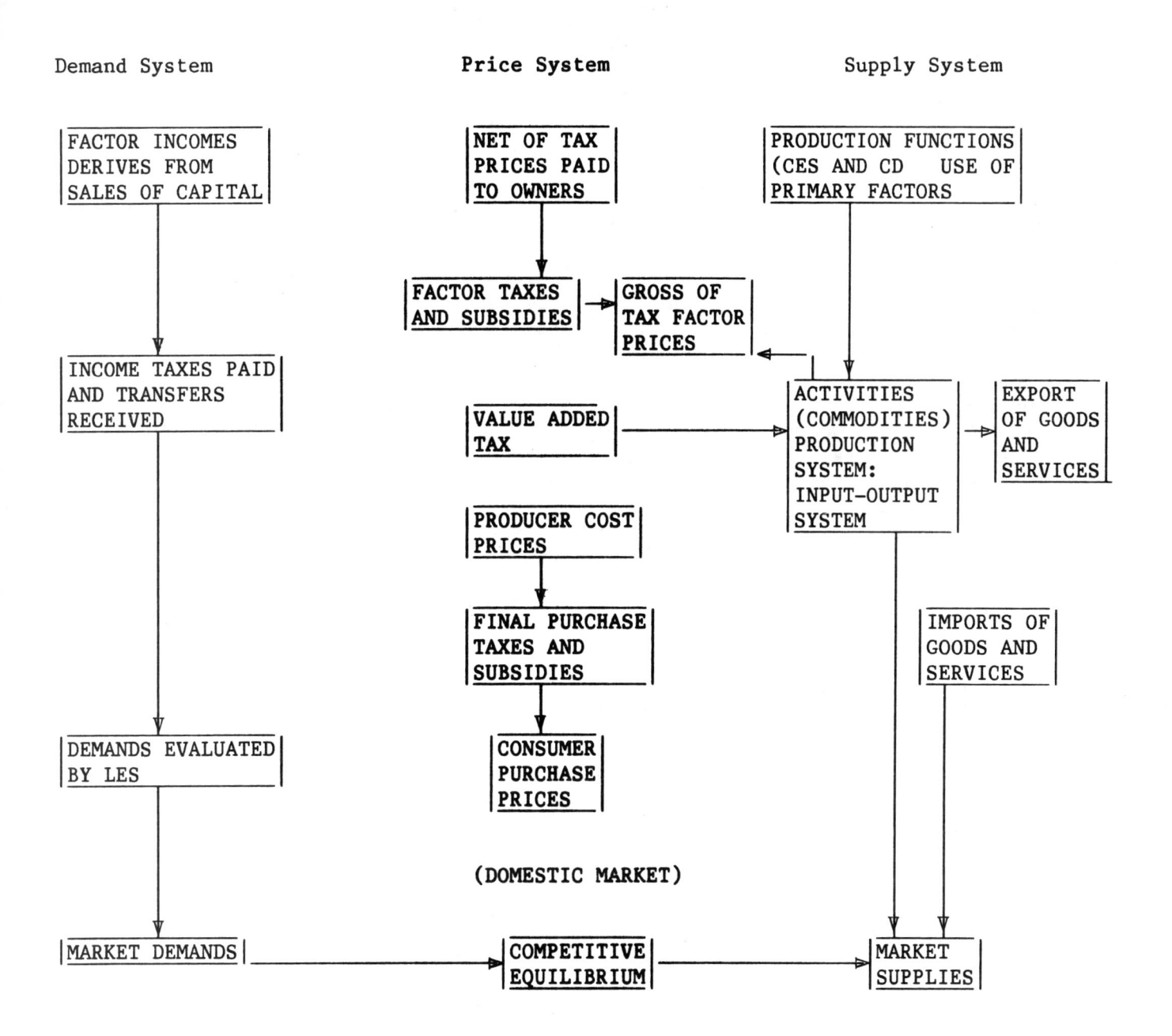

Demand System	Price System	Supply System
FACTOR INCOMES DERIVES FROM SALES OF CAPITAL	NET OF TAX PRICES PAID TO OWNERS	PRODUCTION FUNCTIONS (CES AND CD USE OF PRIMARY FACTORS
↓	↓	↓
INCOME TAXES PAID AND TRANSFERS RECEIVED	FACTOR TAXES AND SUBSIDIES → GROSS OF TAX FACTOR PRICES	
	VALUE ADDED TAX →	ACTIVITIES (COMMODITIES) PRODUCTION SYSTEM: INPUT-OUTPUT SYSTEM → EXPORT OF GOODS AND SERVICES
↓	PRODUCER COST PRICES ↓ FINAL PURCHASE TAXES AND SUBSIDIES ↓ CONSUMER PURCHASE PRICES	IMPORTS OF GOODS AND SERVICES
DEMANDS EVALUATED BY LES		
↓	(DOMESTIC MARKET)	↓
MARKET DEMANDS	— COMPETITIVE EQUILIBRIUM —	MARKET SUPPLIES

sector. Second, there might be important differences in quality or impediments to trade (regulations, quotas, etc.) in several of the products that compose the sector. These reasons explain why there is no excessive specialization in the production structure of most developing countries. If this was the case we would observe a small number of tradables being produced and exported and all the other tradables being imported by a given country[1].

45. The model assumes a Leontief technology among all intermediate goods and labor. This assumption might be justified in the short-run, since there is limited possibility of substitution among those factors. The constant coefficients of production for intermediate products are given by the input-output table of the base year, and it is assumed that the labor coefficients remain constant.

46. However, all the variable factors (intermediate products, labor and imports) are assumed to be substitutable for the fixed factor (capital). Capital is assumed to be immobile across sectors. In certain sectors where there is capacity of production not used, the supply curve would be horizontal and determined by the unit cost of the sector. This means that there are constant average costs in the sector. According to Diagram 2 variable factors are supplied with capital to activities. Activities use these inputs with trade margins to produce goods. Joint production is allowed among activities to produce goods. Commodities are then taxed at the final stage and delivered to the domestic market or exported. Sales taxes are paid at this stage. The value added tax is paid at the activities - goods stage.

47. Table 2.1 shows the classification of activity sectors and the correspondence with the Moroccan nomenclature of economic activity (NMAE). The Social Accounting Matrix is disaggregated in 40 sector of activity. The core model aggregates those activities in 12 sectors.

DIAGRAM 2

SUPPLY DIAGRAM

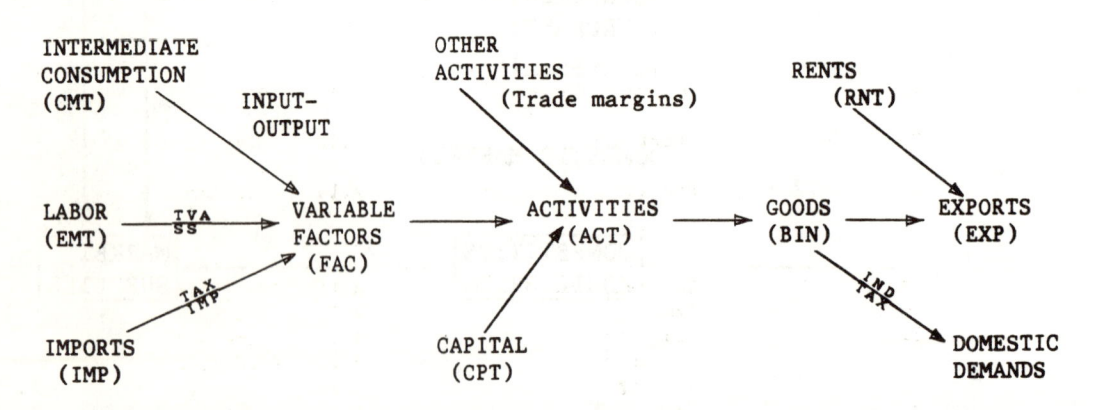

```
INTERMEDIATE              OTHER
CONSUMPTION               ACTIVITIES              RENTS
(CMT)         INPUT-      (Trade margins)         (RNT)
              OUTPUT
                          ↓                       ↓
LABOR    TVA   VARIABLE   ACTIVITIES   GOODS      EXPORTS
(EMT)    SS →  FACTORS →  (ACT)     →  (BIN)  →   (EXP)
               (FAC)                      IND
         TAX                              TAX
         IMP   ↑             ↑             ↘
IMPORTS                   CAPITAL                DOMESTIC
(IMP)                     (CPT)                  DEMANDS
```

---

[1] See A. Kruger, Growth, Factor Market Distortions and Patterns of Trade among Many Countries. Princeton Studies in International Finance, no.40, 1977.

Table 2.1: CLASSIFICATION OF ACTIVITY SECTORS

NMAE	No.	40 Sector Model	12 Sector Model	
01.1	1.1	Cereals	A.1	Cereals
01.2.4	1.2	Sugar	A.2	Sugar
0.1.3	1.3	Citrus fruits	A.3	Agriculture exports
0.1.4	1.4	Vegetables	A.3	Agriculture exports
02	1.5	Meat dairy	A.4	Other agriculture
03	1.6	Fishing	A.4	Other agriculture
0.1.5/ 0.1.6 1.2.0/1.23	1.7	Forest and others	A.4	Other agriculture
0.4.2 04	2	Phosphate	A.5	Phosphates
others	3	Other minerals non metals	A.10	Intermediate and producer industries
05	4	Metal minerals	A.5	Phosphates
06	5	Coal	A.6	Oil and gas
06/07	6	Oil and gas	A.6	Oil and gas
08	7	Electricity and water	A.11	Protected sector
10	8	Food industries	A.7	Food industries
11	9	Otherfood industries	A.9	Export industries
12	10	Beverages and tobacco	A.8	Other consumption industries
13	11	Textiles	A.8	Other consumption industries
14	12	Clothing	A.9	Export industries
15	13	Leather and shoes	A.9	Export industries
16	14	Wooden products	A.8	Other consumption industries
17	15	Paper and printing	A.8	Other consumption industries
18	16	Cement	A.10	Intermediate and producer industries
19	17	Iron and steel	A.10	Intermediate and producer industries
20	18	Metalomecanics	A.10	Intermediate and producer industries
21	19	Machinery	A.10	Intermediate and producer industries
22	20	Transportation material	A.10	Intermediate and producer industries
23	21	Electrical material	A.10	Intermediate and producer industries
24	22	Office machinery	A.10	Intermediate and producer industries
25	23	Chemicals	A.10	Intermediate and producer industries
26	24	Rubber and plastics	A.10	Intermediate and producer industries
27	25	Other industries	A.10	Intermediate and producer industries
29	26	Construction	A.11	Protected
30/2	27	Trade	A.11	Protected
33.5	28	Transports	A.11	Protected
36	29	Communications	A.11	Protected
37	30	Banking	A.11	Protected
38	31	Insurance	A.11	Protected
39/48	32	Trade and other services	A.11	Protected
49	33	Non-market activities	A.12	Administration
37	34	Other banking	A.11	Protected

DIAGRAM 3

DEMAND DIAGRAM

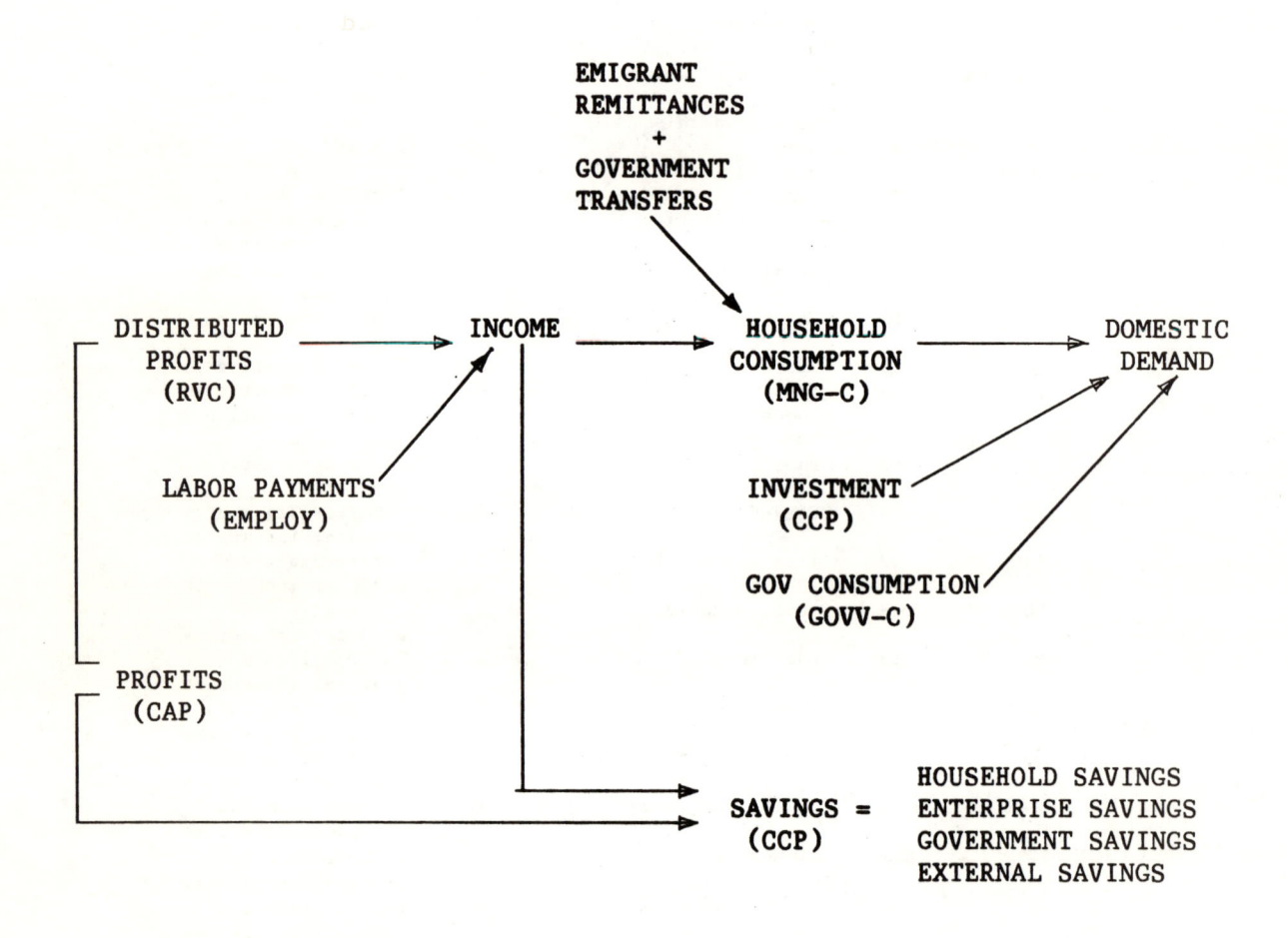

```
                          EMIGRANT
                          REMITTANCES
                              +
                          GOVERNMENT
                          TRANSFERS
                              |
                              v
  DISTRIBUTED  -->  INCOME  -->  HOUSEHOLD     -->  DOMESTIC
  PROFITS                        CONSUMPTION         DEMAND
  (RVC)                          (MNG-C)
    |
    |     LABOR PAYMENTS
    |     (EMPLOY)
    |                            INVESTMENT
    |                            (CCP)
    |
    |                            GOV CONSUMPTION
    |                            (GOVV-C)
    |
  PROFITS
  (CAP)
    |
    |                                         HOUSEHOLD SAVINGS
    +------------------->  SAVINGS =          ENTERPRISE SAVINGS
                           (CCP)              GOVERNMENT SAVINGS
                                              EXTERNAL SAVINGS
```

2.3 The Demand side and Consumption Income Distribution

48. Households are disaggregated into four groups: agricultural households; urban workers households; semi-skilled workers households and higher income households. Consumption behavior is determined by a Linear Expenditure System based on a Stone-Geary utility function. Households spend their income first on the subsistance levels of consumption and then allocate the remaining income among the different goods according to a marginal spending coefficient. Investment has been split between household investment (housing), government investment, and enterprise investment (including public enterprises). Both government and enterprise investment are exogenous. Government consumption in the form of wages and salaries is exogenous, but intermediate consumption in the form of goods is incorporated as a row of the input-output matrix (Diagram 3).

49. Household income derives from different sources: labor payments, distributed profits, and transfers. Labor is paid by enterprises and has to pay a labor tax at the same time. Profits pay first the corporate tax. They are then either distributed to households or retained in a corporate account of enterprises. Part of the profits generated by the phosphate sector (OCP) are paid out to the government and other public enterprises either transfer revenues to the government or receive current subsidies. Households receive transfers from the government, from abroad (emigrants' remittances), and from the Social Security System.

50. Savings have to equal investment by the Walras' law. Household savings are a residual equal to the income not spent. Enterprise savings are the corporate retained profits. Government savings are equal to the current surplus and external savings are equal to the current account deficit of the balance of payments.

2.4 Market Adjustment in Traded and Non-traded Goods Market

51. One of the central characteristics of a computable general equilibrium model is the specification of market adjustment in each of the activity sectors. Is the price flexible? Is the domestic price independent from world trade? Is the supply curve exogenous or is it horizontal? Is the price administered? In this section we are going to explore the alternative specifications of each sector in view of the institutional characteristics of Morocco. In Annex III, the mathematical formulation of each case is presented.

   (a) **Sector Type I** (Agricultural Exports; Agriculture-Others)

52. For this sector, domestic prices adjust to balance supply and demand. Since in this sector commodities have large price differentials vis-a-vis the world prices, either due to transportation costs (e.g. live cattle), protection through quantitative restrictions, or differences in quality (e.g. fresh meat versus frozen meat), there is some isolation from world markets. As Diagram 4 shows, there is a differencial between domestic (P_i^D) and international prices (P_i^W), and the domestic price clears the aggregate demand and supply markets. In the case of agricultural exports there is a large subsector (citrus) where production depends on plantations available. For this sub-sector, in the short-run, there is a low elasticity

of substitution on the production side. On the other hand, for vegetables (tomatoes, legumes) there is a significant elasticity of substitution between capital and other variable factors of production. The calibration of the model reveals a significantly high elasticity of substitution in this sector. The same can be said of the Agriculture-Others sector, where cattle, poultry, milk, forestry, fishing, legumes and pulses are aggregated. From the import side, an Armingtonian formulation is imposed with a low elasticity of substitution between domestic products and imports. Two alternative formulations are advanced for exports. In the first case, a downward-sloping demand curve is stipulated, where exports depend on the price in the domestic market relatively to the world price. In a second case, exports are exogenous and sold at the world price to reflect the existence of a quota in the dominant external market (EEC) due to the Common Agricultural Policy. In the case of exports being sold at a different price (world price) from the domestic price there is a rent generated by exports.

DIAGRAM 4: DEMAND-SUPPLY ADJUSTMENT

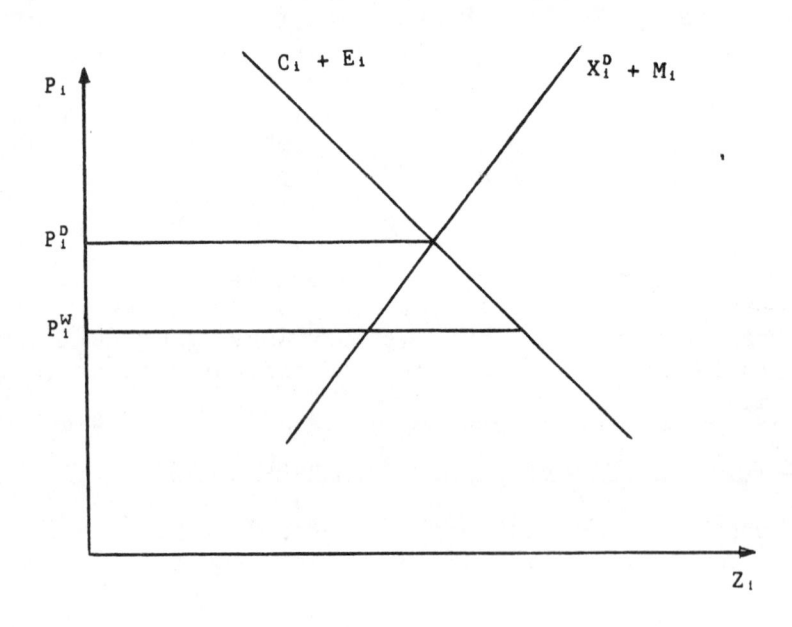

(b) Sector Type II (Cereals)

53. In the cereals sector, we assume that in the short-run production is exogenous, essentially determined by weather conditions. However, in the medium-term, it can be specified with elastic supply (our econometric estimates give a medium term elasticity of about 1). In the short-run, we modelled two types of market adjustment. In the first one, domestic prices adjust to clear the market. There is limited substitution between imports and domestic production because a significant part of cereals production remains in the subsistence sector. In this case there is a divergence between domestic and world prices. The situation where the government imposes quotas on imports and exports falls in the first case and can be represented by Diagran 4. The second case is one of free domestic market where supply is exogenous, domestic prices are determined by world prices and imports are determined by the difference between domestic demand and supply.

Exports continue to be exogenous. This is an alternative market scenario currently being discussed in the Moroccan agricultural policy where a tariff is likely to be introduced to equalize protection across sectors and substitute for quantitative restrictions (see Diagram 5). In the limit, we assume perfect substitution between domestic production and imports..

DIAGRAM 5: DEMAND-SUPPLY ADJUSTMENT

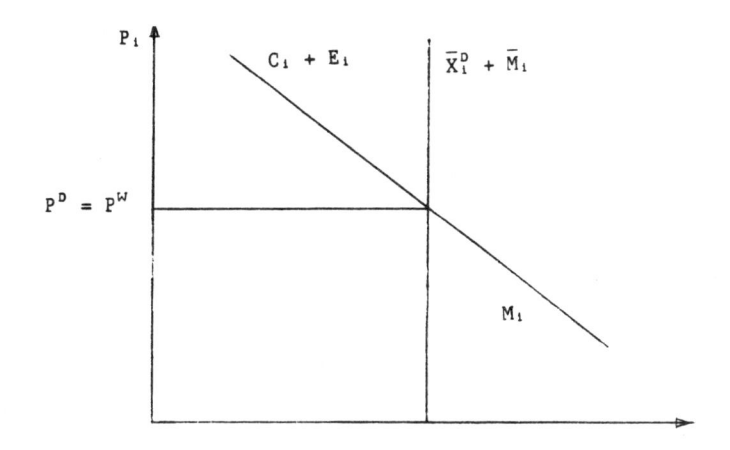

(c) Sector Type III (Food Industries)

54. Prices are controlled in some of the most important food industries (flour, sugar, edible oils). In order to obtain those prices in the market, the government controls exports and imports. In such a market, supply is horizontal (infinitely elastic) and the quantity produced is determined by domestic demand after deducting net imports. On the supply side, we assume that imports are highly substitutable for domestic production and profits are determined as residual (see Diagram 6). An alternative policy regime, currently being discussed, is the case of international price as a reference price for fixing domestic prices and the use of a tariff. In this case, domestic prices would be equal to international prices plus a tariff and net imports (exports exogenous) would be determined by the difference between domestic supply and demand. The supply function depends mostly on agricultural inputs (see Diagram 7).

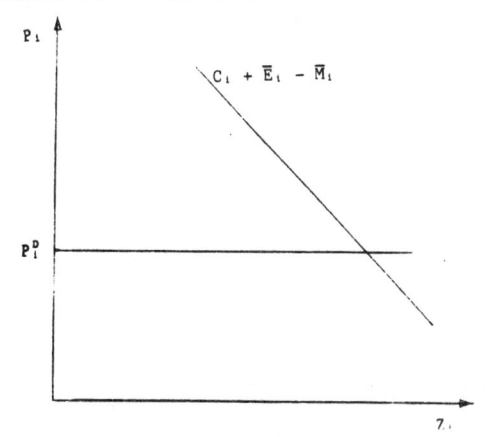

DIAGRAM 6: DEMAND-SUPPLY ADJUSTMENT

DIAGRAM 7: DEMAND-SUPPLY ADJUSTMENT

[Diagram showing axes P_i vs Z_i, with upward-sloping curve C_i, downward-sloping curve X_i^D, horizontal lines at P_i^D (labeled $M_i - \bar{E}_i$) and P_i^W.]

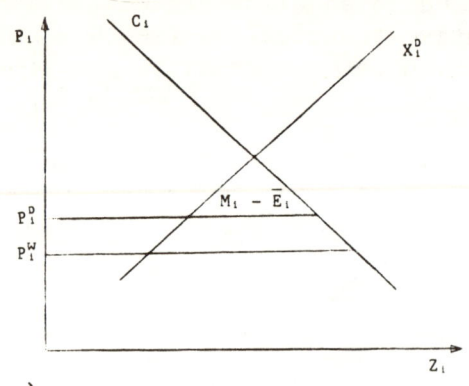

(d) Sector Type IV (Sugar)

55. The agricultural sugar sector presents a special case. The quantity produced is exogenous because the government controls the area cropped with sugar beet and sugar cane. It is also influenced by weather. On the other hand, prices paid to farmers are controlled by the government. Thus, the value of production generated in the sector is fixed. There are no imports or exports and no stocks. All demand is intermediate demand. Thus, any change in quantity demanded would be reflected in change in stocks (see Diagram 8).

DIAGRAM 8: DEMAND-SUPPLY ADJUSTMENT

[Diagram showing axes P_i vs Z_i, with downward-sloping curve C_i, horizontal line at P_i^D meeting vertical at X_i^D.]

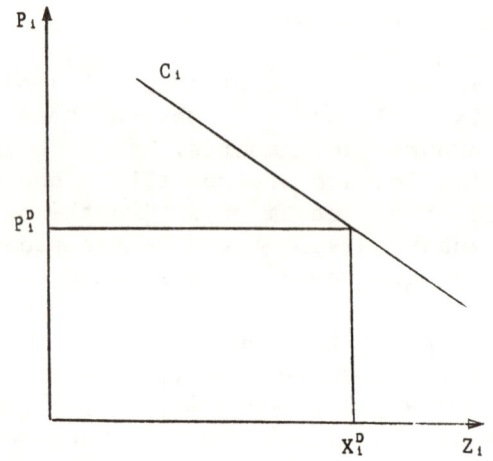

(e) Sector Type V (Industrial Exports)

56. There is limited substitution between domestic production and imports. This substitution is captured by an Armingtonian assumption, and exports confront a downward sloping demand curve. In this case there is a differential between domestic and world prices, that is influenced by taxes and subsidies, the elasticity of substitution between domestic goods, and imports and the export elasticity. Domestic prices (diagram 4) adjusts supply and demand. Capital is fixed and there is significant substitution between fixed and variable factors in the short-run. The wage rate has to be free in order for the supply curve to be upward sloping. The Armingtonian assumption captures the quotas in the sector. Since there are numerous products with different trade regimes, it would be difficult to specify a quota.

57. In a second alternative, the economy is substantially liberalized. Domestic price is now determined by world price plus a tariff. As in the classical model, external trade adjusts the market. There are two submodels in this classical case: in the first, net exports would be fixed and supply would be endogenously determined. In the second, supply is determined exogenously and net exports would be endogenous.

(f) Sector Type VI (Protected and Phosphate Sectors)

58. Inspired by the Scandinavian models of the 1960s, the protected sectors, composed mostly of nontradables, have domestic prices determined by a mark-up formulation. Entrepreneurs compute all the prime costs: labor costs, costs of raw-materials, and costs of imported goods, inclusive of all the commodity taxes and apply a mark-up rate that is assumed to be equal to the one in the base-period. The quantity supplied is determined by demand. If there are imports or exports in some sectors they are determined exogenously.

DIAGRAM 9: DEMAND - SUPPLY ADJUSTMENT

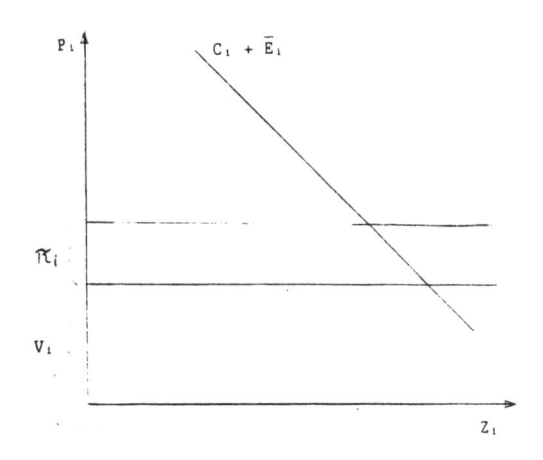

59. Although the typical case of this formulation is a typical nontradable goods, it is possible that for certain tradables sectors the domestic price be different from the international price. Differences in quality between domestic and imported goods or trade restrictions make the good essentially a nontradable and may give the industry a structure of a monopoly or oligopoly. This assumption is used in intermediate and capital goods industries.

60. The phosphate sector, which is a state monopoly, is modelled in the same way. Since Morocco is one of the two main exporters in the oligopoly of phosphate rock world market, exports are considered exogenous and determined by the Moroccan export strategy.

(g) Sector Type VII (Petroleum)

61. Petroleum is one of the largest imports of Morocco. Since there is very limited substitutability among fixed and variable factors of production, a Leontief production function is assumed. We also assume complementarity between imports and intermediate commodities due to the limited substitution between energy and other intermediate goods in the short-run.

DIAGRAM 10: DEMAND-SUPPLY ADJUSTMENT

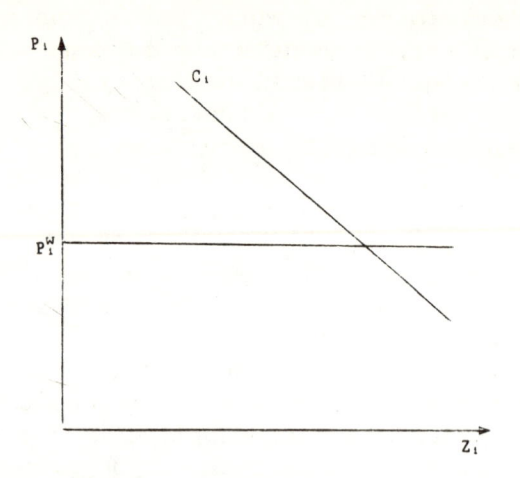

2.5 Equilibrium Solution for the Morocco 85 Model

(a) Short-run

62. The core model of our system of computable general equilibrium models is the Morocco 85 model (code MORC85) that tries to capture the main characteristics of the Moroccan economy in the first half of 1985. Investment and government expenditures are exogenous, nominal wages in the formal sector are fixed. Domestic savings and the deficit of balance of payments are endogenous. The specification that gives the crucial characteristics to the model is the demand-supply adjustment formulated for each sector (see Table 2.2 for details). The main institutional characteristics embedded in the sectoral specification are:

i) the existence of quotas on imports for cereals and the rigidity of production as well as the frequent supply shocks caused by weather;

ii) government regulation of quantities and prices of the sugar agricultural sector;

iii) the existence of quotas in the export markets (EEC) affecting most of the Moroccan agricultural exports [1];

iv) the behaviour of the dominant export of Morocco (phosphate rock) is basically determined by the oligopolistic structure of the world market;

v) prices in the main food industries are controlled and there are import quotas (flour, sugar, tea, edible oils);

vi) industrial exports of textiles and clothing, one of the fastest growing exports, have a high supply elasticity but are subject to intense competition abroad and in the domestic market (due to fluctuations in exchange rate and aggregate demand);

---

[1] Except exports of fresh fish, one of the most successful and rapidly increasing exports to Europe.

vii) intermediate and capital goods industries are relatively isolated from the world market (except phosphate derivatives). These sectors are subject to extensive quotas, tariffs, quality differences, and other interferences to free trade and have essentially a non-competitive environment.

63. This is the model currently being used for policy simulations (see Chapters V through VII). The mathematical formulation of the model is presented in Annex II. The computer program using the SIMS software developed at the World Bank is presented in Annex III, and the data base is the Social Accounting Matrix built for 1985, presented in Annex I.

(b) Long-run

64. The previously described model is a short-run model. Investment is exogenous and there is no feedback from investment to capacity of production. Every growth model recognizes the dual aspect of investment emphasized by Harrod and Domar. When an investment is made, it increases aggregate demand through the keynesian multiplier effect (short-run effect), but it also creates capacity of production that can be used to produce other goods in the future (long-run effect). The long-run model recognizes both effects (see Annex A.III for the mathematical formulation). In this formulation, investment originates from imports or domestic industries producing capital goods and is allocated to the different activity sectors to increase productive capacity. Then productive capacity is linked to output through the production function.[1]

65. The central feature in the allocation process is the mechanism that guides the distribution of investment by sector of destination. Most of the existing computable general equilibrium models specify an exogenous vector of distribution parameters.[2]

66. In the planning models[3] using the dynamic Leontief theory, investment is related to the expected output increase by an accelerator coefficient. However, in the neoclassical theory of investment, the demand for capital goods is related to a measure of profitability of the sector over the cost of new capital goods (Tobin-q). The first formulation can be incorporated easily (see Annex II for the mathematical formulation), but the solution of the general equilibrium model is not easy to compute. The model has to be solved first for the final year, given some target values for the capital stock in the post-planning period. Then the model is solved backwards given a time path for the exogenous variables. The base year solution is then compared with the actual capital stocks and the process is re-started until an acceptable solution is found. The net rate of return of capital should be used to guide the specification of the target structure of capital stocks, assuming that the tendency is for an equalization of the after-tax net rate of profit by industry.

---

[1] The production function is already incorporated in the short-run model.

[2] E.g. the K. Dervis, J. Melo and S. Robinson model.

[3] See L. Taylor, MacroModels for Developing Countries, McGraw-Hill, 1979.

Table 2.2: MOROCCO 85 MODEL

Basic Specification by Sectors of Activity

Agriculture - Exports	Exports exogenous; output endogenous.
Agriculture - Cereals	Output endogenous ; quota on imports; exports exogenous; demand determines domestic price[a].
Agriculture - Sugar	Price and output fixed.
Agriculture - Others	Exports fixed; production endogenous.
Industry - Phosphates	Mark-up; exports exogenous.
Industry - Food	Price fixed; quota on imports; exports exogenous.
Industry - Consumption	Mark-up; exports exogenous.
Industry - Exports	Capital fixed; exports endogenous.
Industry - Capital and intermediate goods	Mark-up; exports exogenous.
Protected Sector	Mark-up; exports exogenous.

[a] In an alternative formulation, production is exogenous and exports endogenous.

2.6 Alternative Model Specifications (Liberalized Economy Model)

67. Nowadays, at the center of the policy debate in Morocco are the effects of liberalization of the economy. What is the impact of an "opening-up" of the economy on GDP, balance of payments and government deficit? The "open-up" involves such policy changes as price liberalization, transformation of quotas into tariffs, abolition of import or export monopolies, and a decrease in the rates of protection.[1] Some of these policies involve a change in policy parameters of the core model. However, and this is the most important aspect of our work, it involves a change in the structure and institutional characteristics of the economy and the model.

[1] The first comprehensive report about these issues is IBRD, Morocco: Export Promotion and Industrial Incentives, 1983.

Since Morocco is a small economy (except for phosphate rock), most of the tradable good prices would be determined by the world price plus a tariff. The difference in quality of certain agricultural and most industrial goods still plays an important role, but as the economy matures, its role should decrease.

68.   Two alternative specifications of the Liberalized Economy Model were tried. The first, so-called Scandinavian type model (A) stipulates mark-up type of adjustment in the nontradable sectors and a flex-price adjustment in all tradable goods, where domestic prices are equal to international prices plus tariffs. The second alternative, the neoclassical specification (B) specifies flex-prices in all sectors where the tradables have the same specification as before, but nontradable prices are not rigid but determined by demand and supply adjustment. In both models, the phosphate sector is specified as in Morocco 85.

Table 2.3:   LIBERALIZED ECONOMY MODEL

Basic Specification by Sectors of Activity

Agriculture - Exports	Output fixed; exports endogenous
Agriculture - Cereals	Output fixed; domestic prices determined by world price plus tariff; exports endogenous.
Agriculture - Sugar	Exports fixed; production endogenous.
Agriculture - Others	Output fixed; exports endogenous
Industry - Phosphates	Mark-up; exports exogenous.
Industry - Food	Domestic price equals to world price plus tariff; imports endogenous; exports exogenous.
Industry - Consumption Goods	Domestic price equal to world price plus tariff; imports endogenous; exports exogenous.
Industry - Exports	Production fixed; domestic price equal to world price plus tariff; exports endogenous.
Industry - Capital and intermediate Goods	Domestic price equal to world price plus tariff; imports and exports exogenous.
Protected Sector	Mark-up; exports exogenous.

69.   Table 2.3 presents the version A of the model and the specification chosen for each sector. Nontradables and phosphates have a mark-up specification. For the traded good sectors, capital is fixed, wage rates are fixed in all formal sectors, quantity supplied of labor is fixed in the informal sector. Then one of the following variables has to be fixed: production, exports, or imports.

70.   In the agricultural sector (except agricultural exports), production is exogenous. In industrial sectors export oriented, exports are chosen endogenously and imports fixed. In most import substitute sectors, imports are chosen endogenously and exports fixed. The closure rule is the same as in the Morocco 85 model. The production structure of each sector is given by a CES.

71.   In the complete neoclassical alternative (B), output prices in the nontradables are also flexible, but both exports and imports that exist in the sector are exogenous. Apart from activities like construction, administration, domestic transportation, trade, and some personal services, there are more and more activities that are subject to international competition . A case in point is the internationalization of services like tourism , banking, and business services that has occurred in the last decade.

72.   One of the most interesting findings of our simulations is how important is in computable general equilibrium models the **specification of the labor market**. The central issue of the controversy in macromodels between keynesians and neoclassicals in the 1960s was the behaviour of the labor market: are nominal wages flexible to adjust the labor market or are there institutional characteristics that lead to its rigidity? In the 1970s, with the advent of rational expectations (neoclassical school) that replaced adaptive expectations, the focus of the controversy moved away from the labor market. However, it has been again recognized in the early 1980s that even assuming rational expectations, price or wage rigidities can lead to unemployment or over-employment phenomena. Our model assumes at most static expectations directly, but the way the labor market is specified has crucial implications in the overall results. If nominal wage rates in the formal sector are fixed, then most of the market adjustment is through quantities and less through prices. If supply of labor is fixed, then the inverse type of adjustment occurs. Notwithstanding further studies of the Moroccan labor market, most of the observers of the economy agree that there is substantial rigidity in nominal wages in a large part of the formal urban labor market. The "efficiency theory" of wages built by Stiglitz to explain the behavior of wages in both formal and informal labor markets of developing countries explains the existence of rigidity even in agricultural labor markets. However, it is clear that in the informal labor markets, nominal wage rates may be more flexible. For these markets where household enterprises are dominant, it is difficult to separate between labor and capital returns.

CHAPTER III

DATA BASE AND CALIBRATION

73. The data base used for calibrating the system of models was a Social Accounting Matrix (SAM) built for 1985, in the tradition of Stone, Pyatt and many others. First a SAM was built for 1980 and later updated for 1985. The basic data set for estimating the SAM for 1980 was the Input-Output Table built by the Statistics Department, Ministry of Planning. Agriculture was further disaggregated in order to analyze issues related to the sector. The total number of activity sectors contained in the present SAM is forty. Data collected by the Food Strategy Group in conjunction with the 1971 Household Survey was used to estimate household consumption by socio-economic groups of population. Four types of households were considered: agricultural, urban low income, urban middle income, and urban high income. The 1982 Population Census, the Urban Employment Survey, and the Industry Survey were all used in estimation of the employment and wages by sector of activity. Employment is disaggregated in raw labor, semi-qualified, technical professions, and managerial and administrative categories. Capital is disaggregated by sector of activity. Lack of data prevented the decomposition of depreciation and net profits. Both labor and capital were further disaggregated into a formal and informal sector.

74. The Public Sector Accounts presented one of the most difficult areas of data manipulation. In fact, a very detailed reclassification of all the items had to be carried out in order to transform the concepts of the Treasury Statistics into National Accounts methodology. First, a full integration of the accounts had to be carried out including Central Government with Local Governments, Special Budgets, Budgets in Annex, and Accounts of Special Institutions like the Stabilization Fund. Social Security was considered a separate institution. Second, quite a number of expenditures included in the capital account had to be transfered to the current account. Finally, since National Accounts measure flow of goods and not treasury positions, an estimate of the arrears in payment by the Treasury had to be included. In order to use the model in simulations of fiscal reform, special care was put in estimation of the tax system. The SAM distinguishes Value Added Taxes, Other Domestic Indirect Taxes, Import Taxes, Corporate Taxes, and Other Direct Taxes. The indirect taxes as well as the corporate tax are decomposed by activity sector. Direct taxes are decomposed by household group.

75. Savings by institution are obtained as a residual from the expenditures-income accounts. Investment was decomposed in household investment in housing, government investment, and enterprise investment in fixed capital and stocks. In the SAM, public enterprises are lumped together with private enterprises.

76. The updating of the SAM for 1985 starts with estimates obtained for the External Sector and Public Sector. It is also based on production and price indices given by the Index of Industrial Production and Wholesale and

Producer Price Indices disaggregated by sectors of activity. For agriculture the estimates for production of the Ministry of Agriculture were used. The algorithm built for updating starts by applying RAS to the input-output and activities table. Household consumption is projected using the Linear Expenditure System estimated. Savings are obtained as a residual.

77. The SIMS software package calibrates the model using the 1985 Social Accounting Matrix as the benchmark. Following most of the CGE models, we used quite standard functional forms for the production and demand systems. For the production system we used CES functions. The lack of data available for its estimation led us to use estimates made for other countries and static simulations to confirm the results. In sectors where evidence pointed for the existence of substantial unused capacity or entry into the market was fairly easy, a relatively high supply elasticity was used. Table 3.1 presents all the elasticities used in the different models. For the demand system, a detailed econometric estimation of a Linear Expenditure System was carried out. The trade elasticities were based on econometric estimates for import and export functions using time series data.

78. This chapter discusses the selection of parameter values for the equations of the model. The approach followed by the SIMS software is to use the equilibrium solution concept of the model and adopt a simple calibration procedure. This calculates parameter values consistent with an assumed equilibrium contained in observed data after adjustments are made to it to ensure all equilibrium conditions hold. We term this a 'benchmark equilibrium.[1]

79. The size of the model and its integrated structure make it impossible to simultaneously estimate all parameter values using conventional simultaneous equation econometric techniques. The number of exogenous variables is small, and extensive use of excluded variables as identifying restrictions is not possible because of the general equilibrium interdependence which the model captures. If, as an alternative, single equation estimation is used, parameter estimates will be obtained which do not necessarily generate an equilibrium consistent with observed data. To achieve this consistency, parameter values for equations were calculated from observed data (after adjustments) using the equilibrium conditions of the model. We utilize this data set along with extraneous elasticity estimates required in our calibration procedure.

80. Since the data used must simultaneously satisfy all model equilibrium conditions, a large amount of work is involved in the construction of a consistent equilibrium data set. In addition, since this data set only yields observations on expenditures, a time dependent units convention was used to separate price and quantity observations. Our units convention makes it difficult to sequence observations for time series estimation even where this is feasible, given the volume of work involved.

---

[1] See J. Piggot, J. Whalley (1985), "UK Tax Policy and Applied General Equilibrium Analysis", Cambridge.

81.   Extraneous estimates of substitution elasticites for both demand and production functions were selected on the basis of some limited estimations and policy experiments. These enter our calibration procedure since our equilibrium observation only generates share parameters for the CES functions we use. 'Second order' substitution parameters must be determined in some other way. For our production function elasticities, we surveyed the literature and did sensitivity analysis. For our demand functions, we estimated a demand system.

82.   This approach to model estimation has important implications for the organization of the basic data used in the study. Obtaining a detailed data set containing production decisions of industries, consumption decisions of households, and taxes paid on transactions, all consistent with the equilibrium solution concept of the model, involved a substantial extension and reorganization of Moroccan economic statistics as currently reported. Some difficulties were associated with collecting raw data in sufficiently disaggregated form. While detailed information is separately available in input-output tables, budget studies, income distribution statistics and other sources, the absence of integrated detailed microeconomic data on consistent classifications, and for the same year, is a major difficulty in a study of this sort. Also, taxation and subsides are relatively neglected in these data, and in places limited detail is available.

3.1 The Choice of Functional Forms for the Behavioral Equations in the Model

83.   Before discussing the estimation of parameter values for the model equations, the considerations involved in the choice of particular functional forms for demand and production functions should be explained. The functional form used in the model must be consistent with the basic model assumptions, and the maximizing responses of agents must be simple enough to make repeated solution in the sequences of calculations involved in equilibrium computations feasible. Tractable functional forms must be used to describe behavior patterns of both producers and consumers.

84.   Inevitably, in practice, a well-known family of convenient functional forms provides the candidate specifications for general equilibrium policy models of the type used here. Demand and cost functions derived from Cobb-Douglas, Stone-Geary, and CES (either single stage or nested) utility and production functions tend to be used. More complex variants (such as Generalized Leontief functions or translogs) may also be considered, although such functions raise more difficult estimation problems and substantially increase execution times required for equilibrium calculations. The choice of CES functions used in this study reflects the trade-off between complexity (and hopefully added realism) and tractability. The use of CES functions (on the demand side nested CES functions) allows corresponding Cobb-Douglas functions to be separately considered as special cases. The CES function is a directly additive function which implies certain restrictions on the corresponding demand functions.

3.2 Alternative Approaches to Parameter Selection

85.   In the model considered here, production functions yield industry costs functions, and the system of demand function has implicitly a Stone-Geary utility function. If we think of a reduced form for the model represented by interdependent excess demand functions, estimation of a conventional form becomes difficult. For the parameters of any particular structural equation to be identified, a large number of excluded exogenous variables or other identifying restrictions are required. This makes identification of all equations in the model by conventional methods (such as zero or other parameter value restrictions) impractical.

86.   One approach to overcome these problems is to partition the model. Production and demand (utility) functions could be separately estimated, and the parameter values introduced into the model. Alternatively, a literature search could be used for parameter selection for some or all portions of the model (such as the demand functions). The major difficulty with this type of procedure is that, in estimating production and demand equations, the exogeneity of variables not central to the equation(s) being considered is assumed; and the estimates so determined are then used in a model which explicitly recognizes their joint endogeneity. There is no guarantee that a model estimated in this way will generate an equilibrium that is at all plausible. In a model which is to be regarded as representative of an actual economy, some overall criterion of reasonableness directly linked to the equilibrium solution concept of the model seems desirable. In the division and reassembly involved in the partitioning of the model for estimation to proceed, no such criterion can be incorporated. It is quite possible, for instance, that an equilibrium could be generated by the model from the estimated parameters in which 30 percent of the labor force is employed in agriculture, when the published statistics suggest that the figure is closer to, say, 12 percent. In addition, partitioning produces difficulties with the compatibility of units used in the general equilibrium model and separate estimation exercises.

87.   For all these reasons, partitioning and separate estimation alone is not adopted here as an approach to parameter selection. Instead, the equilibrium solution concept of the model is used as the primary restriction in the process of parameter selection.

88.   The fundamental assumption made in "calibrating" the model is that the economy is in equilibrium in a particular year. By modifying the National Accounts and other blocks of data for that year, a data set is generated in which all equilibrium conditions inherent in the model are satisfied. This is termed a "benchmark equilibrium" data set. The requirement that the set of parameter values used in the model be capable of replicating this "observed equilibrium" as an equilibrium solution to the model is then imposed as a restriction in the process of parameter selection.

89.   Parameter values are determined in a non-stochastic manner by solving the equations which represent the equilibrium conditions of the model. We use the data on prices and quantities which characterize the benchmark equilibrium. Whether the observed equilibrium alone is sufficient

to determine the parameter values depends upon the functional forms used. For example, Cobb-Douglas functions imply constant shares. The benchmark equilibrium data set, which contains equilibrium share observations, can therefore be generated by only one set of Cobb-Douglas functions. In using CES production and demand functions, extraneous estimates of elasticities of substitution (which are unit free) are incorporated into the procedure, serving together with the equilibrium replication requirement as identifying restrictions on the model.

90. Once functional forms are chosen for production functions, it is possible to calculate the associated distribution parameters by using the benchmark equilibrium observations of capital and labour services used in each industry. The CES value added functions for each industry are given by

$$Y_j = [\delta_j k_j^{-\rho_j} + (1-\delta_j) L_j^{-\rho_j}]^{\frac{1}{\delta_j}}$$

where δ_j is a weighting parameter, and $\delta_j = 1/(1+\rho_j)$ is the elasticity of substitution.

91. For the benchmark equilibrium data set, values for K_i and L_i can be obtained and factor tax rates t_i^K and t_i^L calculated. As units are chosen for productive factors such that $P_K = P_L = 1$ (where P_K and P_L refer to the net of tax factor prices) at the benchmark equilibrium, prices associated with the equilibrium quantities are known.

92. Once a value of δ_j is selected for each industry, the values of δ_j are given by

$$\delta_j = \left[\begin{array}{c} K_j^{\frac{1}{\delta_j}} (1+t_j^K) \\ L_j^{\frac{1}{\delta_j}} (1+t_j^L) \end{array} \right] \left[\begin{array}{c} (+K_j^{\frac{1}{\delta_j}} (1+t_j^K) \\ L_j^{\frac{1}{\delta_j}} (1+t_j^L) \end{array} \right]$$

values for $_j$ are then derived from the zero profit conditions for each industry (given the units definition for outputs).

93. Parameters for household demand function are calculated in a similar manner from the benchmark equilibrium data on purchases of commodities by households.

94. The demand system used in the core model is the Linear expenditure system (LES), based on the Stone-Geary utility function:

$$u(x) = \prod_{k=1}^{n} (x_L - \alpha_K)^{\beta_K}$$

or, in logarithmic form:

$$u(x) = \sum_{k=1}^{n} \beta_K \log (x_k - \alpha_L)$$

Maximizing this utility function subject to the budget constraint gives the system of linear expenditure functions:

$$P_i x_i = P_i \alpha_i + \beta_i (y - \sum_{L+1}^{n} P_k \alpha_k)$$

with $\sum^n \beta_k = 1$, $\beta_k > 0$ and $x_i > \alpha_i$ for all i. This system of demand functions satisfies the "adding-up" homogeneity and symmetry conditions. The well known interpretation is that α_i are the subsistence levels of consumption and $y - \Sigma P_k \bar\alpha_k$ is the "supernumerary expenditure after the subsistence consumption has been satisfied.

95. One of the advantages of the LES is the fact that is has only 2n parameters, (2n-1) of which may be chosen independently. This is because the selection of functional form is itself restrictive. As a draw back, there cannot be inferior goods and all goods are substitutes if the utility function is concave. Even more severe is the Pigou Law[1] verified by all additive function, to which class the LES belongs, if the number of goods - or commodity groups in the case of block additivity - is at all large (in practive more than 8-10 goods), then there is an approximate proportionality of expenditure (e_{ii}) and price elasticities (e_i) $e_{ii} \cong \phi e_i$. In fact, the LES does not measure accurately cross-price elasticities. Yet, is one of the simplest demand systems to implement.

96. The LES was estimated by using a pooling regression of time-series (1970-80) and cross-section (1971 Survey) data using the maximum likelihood Method. However, since we did not have data disaggregated by household (micro data), we had to revert to a calibration estimation of the system of demand function by the four types of household. Let us consider the household type H. From the estimation of the LES (Section 6.4) we obtained the per capita levels of minimum consumption, α_K. Next, we multiplied α_K by the number of persons in each household type (Section 6.4) to obtain α_K^H for each good. If we sum all the subsistence expenditures by household H, then the β's can be computed using the following formula:

$$\beta_i^H = \frac{P_i x_i^H - P_i \alpha_i^H}{y^H - \sum_{K=1}^{\hat{n}} P_K \alpha_K^H}$$

Since $\sum^n \beta_L^H = 1$, the last β_K^H is computed as a difference to 1. The process of calculation is repeated for all types of household H.

3.3 The Construction of a Benchmark Equilibrium Data Set

97. The assumption that an economy is in equilibrium implies that the model equilibrium conditions must be satisfied in any data used to determine parameter values. In a benchmark equilibrium data set, all equilibrium conditions are satisfied. Demands equal supplies for all goods and factors.

98. In order for these equilibrium conditions to be satisfied by the data, various adjustments are necessary. The blocks of data we use are available separately in National Accounts and related sources, but are not

---

[1] See Deaton (1974), A Reconsideration the Empirical Implications of Additive Preferences, Economic Journal, vol 84, 338-48.

arranged on any synchronized basis. These data sets are modified so as to become mutually consistent with each other. In certain cases, prior changes are made to basic data clearly at variance with the model before mutual consistency adjustments to data blocks are undertaken. Table 4.1 presents an example of a simplified benchmark data set in which the model equilibrium conditions are satisfied. We incorporate all tax and subsidy policies into this data set, along with public sector activity.

99. The data requirements for our benchmark equilibrium data set are extensive, and a substantial amount of work was involved in constructing such a set. Data are needed on the use of productive inputs by industry, including the use of both domestic and imported commodities. On the demand side, information is required on the expenditure patterns of different consumer groups and on the composition of their incomes. To incorporate the public sector into the model, data are required on tax revenues, tax payments by agent, subsidy receipts, and transfers; and all as they relate to each producer, commodity, and consumer. Data on government expenditures on goods and services and on foreign trade data are also required. The sources for these data are generally the publications or unpublished records of government agencies, and the methods of manipulation and adjustment are frequently complex. Adjustments are needed for a number of reasons, such as unsuitable stock flow distinctions appearing in the published accounts, incomplete detail on taxes and subsides, differences of definition between source materials and concepts appearing in the model, and classification incompatibilities between the model and basic data sources.

100. The most critical adjustments occur when inconsistent classifications are matched. Information on commodity expenditures by different household groups obtained from survey data is collected on a commodity basis different from the Standard Industrial Classification on which the Input-output Table are based, or the Standard International Trade Classification on which foreign trade statistics are based. Extensive adjustments were thus required.

3.4 Production Function and Trade Elasticities

101. Elasticity values are critical parameters in determining impacts of policy changes generated by the model, and careful discussion of their values is needed prior to presentation of results. We separately report and discuss elasticity values we use for production functions, demand functions, and foreign trade behavior. Our model incorporates CES value added functions for each industry. We therefore need to specify a separate value for the elasticity of substitution between capital and labour for each industry in the model. Since the introduction of the CES function in the early 1960s, there has been a continuing debate as to whether the elasticity of substitution for manufacturing industry is approximately unity. If unity is a correct value, the more complex CES form can be replaced by the simpler Cobb-Douglas form which has unitary elasticity of substitution. This debate has concentrated primarily on substitution elasticities for aggregated manufacturing rather than component industries as specified in the model. This issue is nonetheless important in assessing our choice of values.

102. Early estimation of the elasticity of substitution in manufacturing industry by Arrow, Chenery, Minhas, and Solow (ACMS) (1961), involved a pooled cross country data set of observations on output per man and wage rates for a number of countries. Following ACMS, a number of econometric studies have estimated substitution elasticites for manufacturing industries (primarily in the US) by a number of methods and produced results with substantial variation. Cross-section studies, many of which use statewide data produce estimates which are close to unity, but time-series studies produce lower estimates typically differing from cross-section by a factor of around 2. Also, estimates of substitution elasticities appear to vary systematically with the choice of estimating equation. Using the marginal product of capital relationship produces lower estimates than using the marginal product of labour.

103. The non-existence of time series for labor, capital, and value added by industry precludes any time-series estimation of production in Morocco. Central tendency tables have been produced for elasticity estimates by industry. These have been constructed using a catalogue of industry estimates of substitution elasticites recently compiled by Caddy (1976).[1] They are compiled for all estimates in a given industry, separately for cross-section and time-series estimates, and are shown in Table 4.2.

104. A central set of elasticity values is selected around which sensitivity analysis is conducted. For industries not covered in the central tendency tables, elasticity values fo 1.0 have been assumed (Cobb-Douglas). In the case of the two housing industries, lower values of 0.25 have been used; both of these industries are so overwhelmingly capital intensive that the value used for the substitution elasticities are not of as much consequence as the first sight might appear. It is important to emphasize that these elasticity values represent technological relationships, and when alternative general equilibria are calculated for policy variations, the adjustments between equilibria are assumed to be complete. An assumption of smooth substitutability between capital and labor services in any industry in the short run is clearly not appropriate. Much capital is industry specific and cannot be easily adapted for alternate uses. Complete substitution only takes place in the longer run as capital depreciates and is not replaced. Some adjustments between equilibria may be relatively small and capable of being made quickly, others may require much longer periods of time. The time scale for the model is left ill-defined in terms of a precise number of years. It is assumed that sufficient time elapses for all adjustments between equilibria to be complete and that the counterfactual equilibrium can be achieved under the alternative policy regime as a long-run equilibrium solution.

---

[1] Caddy, V. (1976), "Empirical Estimation of the Elasticity of Substitution: A Review", Melbourne, Australia.

105.   As stated earlier, products produced in Morocco and the rest of the world are treated as qualitatively different while being substitutes in demand. This implies that substitution elasticities between domestic and foreign goods in Morocco can be chosen to calibrate to estimates of import price elasticities, while comparable substitution elasticities in the rest of the world can be chosen to calibrate to estimates of Morocco export price elasticities. The most complete set of estimates of trade elasticities is the recent compendium compiled by Stern, Francis and Schumacher (SFS) (1976)[1]. They briefly summarize the results of approximately 150 empirical studies from the period 1960-1975 which estimate trade elasticities by product and by trading area. They report the main finding of each study and produce central tendency tables from which they extract best guess estimates. They suggest that there is little basis on which to produce best guess estimates on a more detailed product classification than single digit SITC categories, and they also stress the small sample size for estimates for countries other than the US. Their uncompensated price elasticity estimates for Morocco are -0.65 for import demand and -0.48 for export demand.

106.   The estimates for both import and export price elasticities summarized in SFS strike many people as surprising low. There has been extensive discussion of bias in estimates based on time series data following Orcutt's well known paper (1950), and further papers by Kemp (1962) and Kakwani (1972) have provided arguments as to why trade elasticities might be biased towards -1. Some authors argue for and use substantially higher trade elasticities based on so-called "tariff elasticities". Balassa and Kreinin (1967), for instance, in their empirical work on Kennedy Round tariff cuts, use significantly higher elasticities in absolute value. Some recent literature has suggested that the problems of bias first raised by Orcutt may not be as serious as once supposed and estimates in the range reported by SFS, remain both widely accepted and widely used.

107.   Table 3.1 summarizes the evidence thus far assembled through econometric estimations for trade elasticities in Morocco. As the results show, a fundamental distinction has to be made between short-run and long-run elasticities. For most of the cases, long-run price elasticities are substantially higher than the short-run. One striking result is the relatively high long-term supply elasticity for manufactured exports. These elasticities are influenced by the trade restrictions in place and its variations over time. Table 3.2 summarizes the supply and trade elasticities used in the three models of the Moroccan economy. These elasticities take into consideration not only the evidence thus far assembled, but also the static simulations presented in Parts I and II.

---

[1] R. Stern, J. Francis and B. Schumacher (1976), Price Elasticities in International Trade, McMillan.

3.5 Estimation of the Demand System

Estimation of a 8-product system using the classification of the input-output table

108. The estimation of the LES using a 8-product aggregation for the core model, uses the following industry classification:

1. Agriculture - exports sector (AGREXP)
2. Agriculture - import substitutes sector (AGRIMP)
3. Agriculture - protected sector (AGRPROT)
4. Petroleum - (PETROL)
5. Industry - exports sector (INDEXP)
6. Industry - import substitutes sector (INDSVBS)
7. Industry - imports sector (INDIMP)
8. Protected sector (PRO)

Table 3.1: TRADE ELASTICITIES FOR MOROCCO

		Price Elasticity SR	Price Elasticity LR	Income Elasticity SR	Income Elasticity LR	Source
I.	**Imports of goods and services**					
	Overall	.30	.60	1.30		(1)
	Consumption goods	.95	1.70	.76	1.33	(2)
	Intermediate goods	.33	1.21	*		(2)
	Investment goods	.67	.74	1.38	*	(2)
II.	**Exports of goods and services**					
	Overall (demand)		1.63		1.24	(1)
	Agricultural goods (supply)		.76		–	(3)
	Phosphates (demand)	.00	.40	1.02	*	(3)
	Manufactured goods (supply)	.71	2.7		–	(3)
III.	**Tourist receipts** (demand)	1.50	1.80		1.48	(3)
IV.	**Emigrants' remittances**	2.0[4]		1.3		(3)

Sources:
(1) A. Mateus, A Macroeconometric Model for Stabilization Policies in LDC's: The Case of Morocco; 1985.
(2) R. Faini, Import Demand and Non Tariff Barriers: an Application to Morocco; 1986.
(3) Morocco: Industrial Incentives and Export Promotion, IBRD, 1983.
(4) Real interest rate elasticity

* Means non-significant.

Table 3.2: SUPPLY AND TRADE ELASTICITIES

MORC85B

	SUPPLY FIX	SUPPLY ELASTICITY	IMPORTS FIX	IMPORTS ELASTICITY	EXPORTS FIX	EXPORTS ELASTICITY
AGREXP		.2		.2	Q	1.3
AGR-CE	Q		Q	INF		INF
AGRP-S	PQ	.2				
AGRP-O	Q	1.2		.8		2.5
PHOSPH		.2		.2	Q	INF
PETROL				EPS	Q	INF
INDEXP	CAPITAL	1.5		.8		2.5
INDS-F	P	.4	Q	3.	Q	INF
INDS-O		.4		3.	Q	INF
INDIMP		.2		.2		2.5
PROTEC				.2	Q	INF
ADMINS						

LIBL85A

	SUPPLY FIX	SUPPLY ELASTICITY	IMPORTS FIX	IMPORTS ELASTICITY	EXPORTS FIX	EXPORTS ELASTICITY
AGREXP	CAPITAL	.9		.4		1.3
AGR-CE	CAPITAL	.8		.9		3.0
AGRP-S	CAPITAL	.4				
AGRP-O	CAPITAL	.8		.6		2.5
PHOSPH		.2		.2	Q	INF
PETROL	CAPITAL	.4		EPS	Q	INF
INDEXP	CAPITAL	1.1		1.2		2.5
INDS-F	CAPITAL	.7		3.		3.0
INDS-O	CAPITAL	.6		3.		3.0
INDIMP	CAPITAL	.4		.4		2.5
PROTEC		.6		.2	Q	INF
ADMINS						

LIBL85B

	SUPPLY FIX	SUPPLY ELASTICITY	IMPORTS FIX	IMPORTS ELASTICITY	EXPORTS FIX	EXPORTS ELASTICITY
AGREXP	CAPITAL	.9		.4		1.3
AGR-CE	CAPITAL	.8		.9		3.0
AGRP-S	CAPITAL	.4				
AGRP-O	CAPITAL	.8		.6		2.5
PHOSPH	CAPITAL	.2		.2	Q	INF
PETROL	CAPITAL	.4		EPS	Q	INF
INDEXP	CAPITAL	1.1		1.2		2.5
INDS-F	CAPITAL	.7		3.		3.0
INDS-O	CAPITAL	.6		3.		3.0
INDIMP	CAPITAL	.4		.4		2.5
PROTEC	CAPITAL	.6		.2	Q	INF
ADMINS						

109. A correspondence with the branches of the Household Consumption Survey is presented in Annex VIII. The demand system uses time series data for the 1970-80 period plus cross section data for a 20 group classification of households by income group. The pooled system was estimated by the Method of Maximum Likelihood:

$$P_i x_i = P_i \alpha_i + \beta_i [y - \sum_{K+1}^{n} P_K \alpha_K] + \delta_i DIM + e_i$$

where the dummy is 0 for a time series observation and 1 for a cross section observation.

110. In the estimation process, some of the α_i's obtained were negative (3 sectors) in the first run, which would violate the conditions imposed by the utility function. For those minimum consumptions, a restriction was imposed that they would equal 90% of the lower per capita consumption observed in the sample. The results are presented in Table 3.3 as well as the income elasticities from the system.

Table 3.3: HOUSEHOLD CONSUMPTION: PARAMETERS OF THE DEMAND SYSTEM USED IN THE MODEL (LES)

	PARAMETERS				INCOME ELASTICITIES			
	AGRICULTURAL HOUSEHOLDS	URBAN WORKERS	INTERMEDIATE INCOME HOUSEHOLDS	HIGH INCOME HOUSEHOLDS	AGRICULTURAL HOUSEHOLDS	URBAN WORKERS	INTERMEDIATE INCOME HOUSEHOLDS	HIGH INCOME HOUSEHOLDS
AGR. EXPORTS	1089.9 / .069	659.5 / .073	106.0 / .052	10.5 / .035	.75	.96	.98	1.02
AGR. CEREALS	1310.8 / .152	2198.4 / .018	441.6 / .004	37.4 / .002	.96	.27	.13	.16
AGR OTHERS	1048.5 / .074	1162.1 / .072	255.7 / .069	22.8 / .053	.80	.79	.89	.97
OIL	115.6 / .011	92.2 / .044	18.9 / .080	71.6 / .076	.88	1.14	1.08	.84
IND.EXP.	1627.9 / .208	1580.8 / .167	354.5 / .128	43.9 / .112	.99	.95	.93	.98
IND. SUBSTITUTES FOOD	989.4 / .056	672.6 / .073	154.3 / .061	29.6 / .030	.72	.96	.95	.83
IND. SUBSTITUTES OTHERS	945.7 / .086	624.8 / .125	143.2 / .158	27.5 / .242	.88	1.05	1.04	1.07
OTHER UNDUSTRIAL GOODS	139.6 / .104	106.3 / .101	23.0 / .095	23.5 / .105	1.30	1.171	1.08	1.03
PROTECTED SECTORS	151.8 / .240	123.1 / .326	24.9 / .353	47.8 / .346	1.35	1.19	1.10	1.06

Note: The first number in each cell is the minimum consumption (α's) and the second is the marginal propensity to consume "super numéraire" income (β's).

111.   One of the most important results of the theory of separability of utility functions is that the way that groups of goods are aggregated matters in terms of estimation of the system. In this section, we used the most current type of disaggregation-aggregation of goods from the theory of consumption. This extended estimation of the demand system allows us to obtain the parameters for a more disaggregated version of the general equilibrium model. We started by disaggregating total household consumption in 7 groups of expenditure:

1. Food
2. Clothing
3. Durable goods
4. Housing
5. Services
6. Transportation
7. Energy

112.   Next food was disaggregated in 10 groups, clothing in 4, durable goods in 7, services in 6, transports in 2 and energy in 2. For each group in each stage of estimation, one of the goods had to be treated as residual in order to satisfy the aggregation condition. Data for estimation is also a pooling of time series (1970-80)[1/] and cross-section data. The same method described in the previous section is followed, and table 3.5 presents the results.

Table 3.4:   COEFFICIENTS OF ESTIMATED DEMAND SYSTEMS AND
INCOME-ELASTICITIES BY TYPE OF PRODUCT
(8 SAM Sectors)

	1	2	3	4	5	6	7	8
i	.0294 (17.3340)	.0237 (4.6019)	.0554 (18.6114)	.0244 (18.4588)	.1168 (19.8603)	.1664 (51.6871)	.0844 (25.8528)	.4995
i	28.170	33.88	27.101	2.339	50.155	50.860	3.732	4.302

	Sector	Estimates of Income-Elasticities
1.	AGREXP	.5591
2.	AGRIMP	.2969
3.	AGRPROT	.6940
4.	PETROL	.7686
5.	INDEXP	.6218
6.	INDSUBS	.7764
7.	INDIMP	1.2087
8.	PRO	1.8307

1/ Except for food that covers 1970-84.

Table 3.5: SYSTEM ESTIMATES OF LES
(1st Level of Aggregation)

Type of product	i	i	Income-Elasticity
1. Food	.2450	153.796	.5589
2. Clothing	.0969	4.526	.9114
3. Durable Goods	.1235	1.713	1.399
4. Housing	.0239	1.173	.9662
5. Services	.4554	4.090	1.6339
6. Transportation	.0399	2.645	.8143
7. Energy	.0154	.463	1.0522

Table 3.5: SYSTEM ESTIMATES OF LES
(2nd Level of Aggregation)

Type of product	i	i	Income-Elasticity
Food Products			
1. Cereal, flour, bread, pasta	.1385	41.472	.5713
2. Citrus	.0277	.246	1.6279
3. Other fruits & preserves	.0599	14.217	.8540
4. Vegetables and legumes	.1086	33.281	.9689
5. Meat	.3443	17.444	1.4571
6. Fish	.0219	4.588	1.1567
7. Sugar	.1235	12.863	1.2619
8. Milk	.0228	6.266	.4736
9. Edible oils	.0311	5.860	.8254
10. Tea, coffee, beverages, salt and others	.1217	9.792	1.0192
Clothing			
1. Other Clothing	.3762	1.045	1.0572
2. Textiles and knits	.4634	2.501	1.0277
3. Leather goods	.1423	.233	1.0249
4. Articles in rubber or plastic	.0181	1.275	.3134

Table 3.5: SYSTEM ESTIMATES OF LES (cont'd)
(2nd Level of Aggregation)

Type of product	i	i	Income-Elasticity
Durable Goods			
1. Furniture	.0922	.765	.5741
2. Ovens, kitchen products	.0528	0	1.1858
3. Cars	.5738	0	1.3907
4. Cements and other construction materials	.0191	.5	.4182
5. Clocks, watches	.0196	0	.6937
6. Radio, TV, electronic material	.1281	0	.7454
7. Other products	.114	.433	.8382
Services			
1. Paper and cardboard	.0804	0	1.7325
2. Chemical products	.1199	1.789	.7287
3. Public services	.7808	2.776	1.0068
4. Telecommunications	.0108	0	1.5270
5. Banking	.0020	0	1.0867
6. Insurance	.0061	0	1.3212
Transportation			
1. Public transportation and maintenance of private cars	.5797	.909	1.2685
2. Gasoline, fuel	.4203	2.071	.7740
Energy			
1. Electricity and water	1.0291	.459	1.2731
2. Coal	-.0291	0	-.1606

PART II: EMPIRICAL ANALYSIS OF STABILIZATION POLICIES

129.	About one hundred simulations with the core model (Morocco 85) model were performed, using the 1985 Social Accounting Matrix (SAM) as the base and the Morocco 85 Model. From those simulations, fifteen were selected to illustrate different policy packages in the areas of stabilization and structural adjustment policies. Table 4.1 summarizes those simulations.

CHAPTER IV

EMPIRICAL EFFECTS OF BUDGETARY/DEVALUATION/WAGE POLICIES AND EXTERNAL SHOCKS

130.	This chapter analyzes the results of model simulations of typical stabilization packages: budgetary policies, devaluation, and income policies. Budgetary policies to reduce the budget and external deficit involve generally: i) cuts in government current expenditures; ii) cuts in government investment; and iii) increases in tax rates. Cuts in government current expenditures could involve several alternatives like: a) reduction in expenditures on personnel; b) cuts in expenditures on goods; c) reduction in food subsidies; or d) reduction in current transfers to enterprises. The change in tax rates has two important effects: the macro effect on aggregate output and employment, and the resource allocation effect. There are also important intertemporal effects in the case of profit taxes. Incomes policies are mainly related with changes in nominal wage rates. Income policies would have relevance in terms of manipulation of minimum wage rates (SMIG and SMAG), public sector wage rates, and characteristics of the wage contracts between enterprises and trade-unions.

133.	The country has a fixed exchange rate system. In our model, devaluation has a restrictive interpretation: the change in the relative price of tradables verus nontradables, or the change in domestic price of all tradables relatively to the international price.

4.1 Empirical Effects of Budgetary Policies

134.	The target of stabilization policies is usually to reduce the external deficit and contain inflation at a minimum cost to growth and employment. One of the primary instruments to reach these objectives is to decrease the government deficit. The first obvious question to ask is by how much the deficit should be reduced? The answer depends on various financing and macroeconomic times. However, in order to clarify the issue we should start by using the relevant concept of deficit. For short-run analysis, the traditional concept of deficit, measuring the borrowing requirements of the Public Sector is generally accepted as the most important one. Most of the analysis favor the broadest concept of Public Sector. In the Moroccan context, a minimum concept would be the Treasury or Central Government, Local Governments, and Social Security System. The broader concept should include the Public Enterprises. For lack of reliable data, we consider only the first domain.

Table 4.1: LIST OF SIMULATIONS PERFORMED
(All simulations take 1985 as the base year)

Number of simulation	Name	Acronymes	Characteristics
1.	Cut government investment	GOVINV-10%	Cut by 10%
2.	Cut government consumption	GOVC-10%	Cut by 10%
3.	Increase commodity taxes	TAXCOM	Increase the tax rates on import and domestic indirect taxes by 10%, ie, $t = t \times 1.1$
4.	Increase corporate taxes	TAXCORP	old tax rates new tax rates Agriculture exempt (same) INDEXP .017 .09 INDS-F .073 .10 INDS-O .028 .09 IND-IMP .037 .12 PROTECT .037 .08
5.	Tax reform and y taxes increase in investment	TAXPOLICY	Increase of 10% in indirect taxes, reduction of 10% in food subsidies, increase in public investment by 5% and increase of 10% in private investment.
6.	Devaluation	DEVAL 10%	Real devaluation, by increasing the foreign prices relative to domestic prices by 10%.
7.	Nominal wage increase	WAGE 10%	Increase in all formal sector wages by 10% including nominal wages in public sector
8.	Oil price shock	OIL	40% decrease in world price of oil
9.	Phosphate price shock	PHOS PRICE	20% increase in world phosphate price
10.	Inward-oriented stabilization package	STABL 3	10% increase import taxes; 30% cut in import quotas (tightening of QRs); 5% cut in government consumption, 20% cut in government investment;
11.	Outward-oriented stabilization package	IMF 1	5% cut government consumption; 10% cut government investment; 10% devaluation;
12.	Trade liberalization	TRDLIB	20% increase import quotas (softening QRs) 10% cut across board import taxes; Increase in trade elasticities
13.	Tax reform	TAXREF	Increase in average tax rates to close the current government deficit, with decrease in import taxes: old tax rates new tax rates (average) (average) Import taxes Domest. Ind. taxes Corporate taxes
14.	Agriculture reform	AGRREF	Elimination consumer subsidies compensated by income transfer to households; Freezing domestic production of sugar; Quota in cereals replaced by 20% tariff rate
15.	Trade liberalization with devaluation	DEVCOMP	Same as above (12) plus a 5% devaluation

135.   However, recent literature has brought to the fore the need to place the concept of the deficit in a medium-term perspective. A first correction advocated by some economists is the correction of interest payments[1] for the erosion of public debt due to inflation. However, as in enterprise accounting, when interest payments are corrected for inflation, also all the other elements of the balance sheet and profit-loss account should be corrected for inflation. Lacking dynamic macroeconomic model, incorporating the portfolio choices among all assets, the concept of <u>structural government deficit</u> has been used as a rule of thumb for shedding light in the adjustment of the Public Sector. Most of the theoretical models show that a persistent positive structural deficit would produce crowding-out. There would be decrease of the long-run capital stock and consequently of income growth and there would be either increase in the structural rate of inflation or increase in the burden of the external debt. Assume a country with a large external deficit. Fluctuations in world inflation, in nominal interest rates, and in exchange rates of the currencies in which the debt is denominated are bound to cause sharp movements in the interest charges of the debt. Moreover, in the case of Morocco, there are large fluctuations in phosphate prices that cause important changes in phosphate government revenues. Finally, taxes and expenditures fluctuate with economic activity, and some may be temporary. To standardize the variables in a medium-run prespective seems a major improvement over the so-called "full-employment deficit" of the 1960s.[2]

136.   The estimates of the structural deficit after debt relief, thus obtained, (Graph 4.1) show that the government was running an unsustainable large deficit from 1974 to 1984 of about 8.2% of GDP. There has been a significant reduction afterwards (3 percentage points of GDP). But the <u>deficit was still clearly unsustainable in 1987</u> (11.6% of GDP before debt relief and 4.9% of GDP after debt relief).

137.   A <u>cut in government spending</u> decreases aggregate demand in the short-term, in a real model. But if there is "crowding-out" there might be some replacement of credit from the public towards the private sector, and the end result is not as clear-cut. In real models, a cut in government investment is reflected in a fall in the orders to capital goods and mostly construction. There is a decrease in imports of capital goods. The decrease in construction activity leads to a decrease in the demand for labor, since it is generally a labor-intensive sector. These effects entail a decrease in real income with the consequent impact on aggregate demand. Now, the spread of these effects to other sectors depends on the price-quantity adjustments of the different sectors and the decomposition of consumption of the expenditure classes suffering mostly from the downturn. A <u>cut in government consumption</u> in the form of reduction of the spending on goods and services as well as a reduction in the public wage bill reduces demand for the activity sectors selling to the public sector and lowers income to the groups working for government. A reduction in aggregate demand follows but its sectoral composition depends

---
[1] See e.g. J. Siegel, "Inflation-induced Distortions in Government and Private Savings Statistics", Rev. Econ. Statistics, 1979; R. Eisner and P. Pieper, "A New View of the Federal Debt and Budget Deficits", A.E.R., 1984.
[2] See W. Buiter, "The Theory of Optimum Deficits and Debt" In Economics of Large Government Deficits, F.R. Bank of Boston, 1983.

GRAPH 4.1

PUBLIC SECTOR DEFICITS

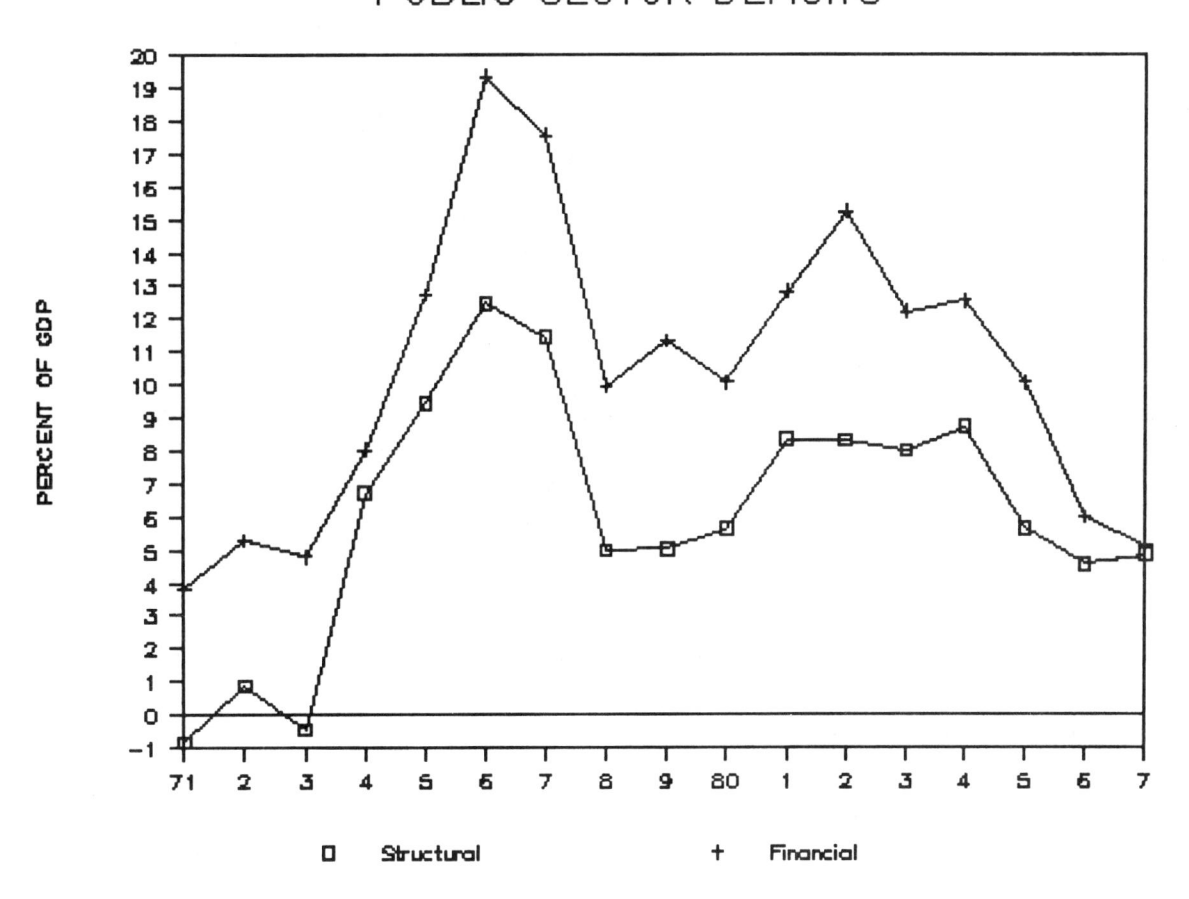

again on the sectoral adjustments. Both policies reduce the external deficit. If the import content of the goods used in public investment is high compared with consumption goods used plus the indirect effects of less labor income, then the first policy has a larger impact on the external deficit. An increase in commodity taxes increases the prices of the goods in the taxed sector, leading to an increase in the price level and a decrease in demand. With nominal wages given, the drop in real income a multiplier effect leads to a decrease in aggregate demand. There is also a decrease in external deficit.

138. A cut in government spending of various sorts may also affect employment, output, consumption, and investment by altering the wealth of the representative agent or by directly affecting the marginal productivity of labor and private capital. An increase in labor-income tax will decrease the consumption in this period and in the near future, and will decrease the overall work effort. This effect will influence mostly marginal groups in the work place (informal versus formal labor participation, women and young workers). On a dynamic framework, labor taxes will increase the cost of labor and over time will decrease the use of labor. However, the decrease in consumption and consequent increase in savings will lead to larger capital accumulation and the increase in capital stock might counterbalance the previous effect. Several economists on development economics have proposed the use of labor subsidies to account for distortions arising from rural-ruban labor cost differential and the occurrence of labor migration à la Harris - Todaro. An increase in profit taxes would lead to a fall in current investment. This occurs because the after-tax rate of return on investment is now reduced. Since current investment falls, the agent uses these extra resources to increase his current consumption and reduce his current labor effort. Future labor supply increases, because the reduction in current investment causes future output and hence consumption to fall. Thus, the fall in future output due to a lower capital stock is partially offset by the agent increasing his labor supply in that period. The model structure does not capture all these interactions since government consumption and investment are independent of private investment. None of these influence labor or capital productivity. So, the results of the simulations must be read with those limitations in mind.

Simulation 1: Cut in government investment by 10%.

140. A cut in civil government investment (see Table 4.2) affects mainly the protected sector and indirectly manufacturing. However, given the already low level of investment, a 10% cut causes only a drop of -.5% of GDP. Assuming that private investment remains the same, the cut in total investment is only of 1.3%. Exports remain the same and private consumption and imports drop half of a percent. In this simulation, investment is cut by DH 392 million, but because tax receipts decrease (current deficit increases by DH 130 million) the total deficit only improves by DH 254 million. The balance of payments improves by about DH 156 million.

Simulation 2: Cut in government consumption by 10%

141. A cut in government consumption, in the form of wages and salaries, leads to a fall of about 4.1% in GDP. The sectors of production most affected are the consumer industries and agricultural goods with high income

Table 4.2: SUMMARY OF STATIC SIMULATIONS

	BASE	Cut Governt Investment	Cut Governt Consumption	Increase Commodity Taxes	Increase Corporate Taxes	Cut Commodity Taxes plus Increase Publ Invest
GDP at constant prices	132591.0	0.995	0.959	0.977	0.969	0.990
Price	1.000	1.001	1.011	1.020	1.010	1.018
Cereals	1.000	0.959	1.010	0.994	1.011	0.989
Agricult Exports	1.000	1.125	1.008	1.000	1.008	0.996
Sugar	1.000	1.000	1.000	1.000	1.000	1.000
Agricult Others	1.000	0.886	1.199	1.144	1.201	1.072
Phosphates	1.000	1.049	0.997	1.008	0.997	1.010
Industr Exports	1.000	1.007	1.048	1.043	1.048	1.026
Food industries	1.000	1.000	1.000	1.000	1.000	1.000
Ind Substit Others	1.000	1.045	0.999	1.015	0.998	1.017
Inter capital goods	1.000	1.057	0.992	1.009	0.992	1.012
Protected sector	1.000	1.056	0.986	1.000	0.985	1.006
Petroleum	1.000	1.104	1.001	1.000	1.001	0.999
Volume						
Cereals	13264.7	1.000	0.997	0.997	0.996	0.998
Agricult Exports	6582.7	0.997	0.972	0.983	0.973	0.991
Sugar	603.6	1.000	1.000	1.000	1.000	1.000
Agricult Others	15976.4	0.991	0.933	0.950	0.930	0.975
Phosphates	8439.8	0.999	0.996	0.995	0.994	0.999
Industr Exports	19320.9	0.994	0.943	0.953	0.943	0.972
Food industries	8866.7	0.996	0.969	0.978	0.969	0.989
Ind Substit Others	16959.2	0.998	0.970	0.978	0.970	0.987
Inter capital goods	24593.6	0.998	0.987	0.985	0.982	0.997
Protected sector	85538.9	0.994	0.977	0.982	0.975	0.994
Petroleum	14565.7	0.997	0.978	0.988	0.978	0.998
Household Consumption	89870.3	0.995	0.956	0.965	0.957	0.977
Price	1.000	1.001	1.015	1.022	1.015	1.018
Volume						
Agr households	26079.6	1.002	1.003	0.985	1.001	0.983
Urban low	43732.9	0.992	0.931	0.953	0.939	0.972
Urban middle	16731.3	0.994	0.946	0.965	0.937	0.980
Urban upper	3326.6	0.995	0.955	0.960	0.942	0.973
Investment	28427.3	0.987	0.999	0.998	0.966	1.037
Exports	26494.9	1.000	0.991	0.984	0.992	0.986
Price	1.000	1.000	1.003	1.006	1.003	1.006
Volume						
Inter capital goods	5411.0	1.005	1.023	0.983	1.024	0.973
Agriculture	1977.0	1.000	1.000	1.000	1.000	1.000
Industrial exp	4013.0	0.990	0.912	0.916	0.912	0.945
Others	9370.9	1.000	1.000	1.000	1.000	1.000
Phosphate minerals	5723.0	1.000	1.000	1.000	1.000	1.000
Imports	39051.7	0.996	0.978	0.980	0.975	0.994
Price	1.000	1.000	1.000	1.000	1.000	1.000
Volume						
Cereals	2799.0	1.000	1.000	1.000	1.000	1.000
Inter capital goods	17222.0	0.996	0.977	0.982	0.971	1.001
Others	3800.7	0.998	0.993	0.979	0.992	0.982
Oil	10673.0	0.997	0.976	0.987	0.977	0.998
Consumer ind	4557.0	0.993	0.961	0.947	0.959	0.963
Government						
Revenues	27783.5	27645.2	27201.6	29065.7	28997.9	29459.3
Current expend	36118	36115.9	34006.7	35882.2	36091.8	35889.2
Capital expend	3837.0	3445.0	3801.6	3862.6	3798.2	4075.1
Deficit global	-10041.5	-9787.8	-8503	-8784.9	-8788.3	-8603.7
Balance payments						
Trade deficit	-12556.8	-12417.6	-11850.6	-12055.1	-11724.9	-12535.5
Current deficit	-6806.7	-6650.8	-6016.1	-6247	-5779.2	-6765.9
Terms of trade	1.000	1.000	1.003	1.006	1.003	1.006
Total employment	43022.9	0.998	0.95	0.989	0.987	0.995

elasticity. Private consumption drops by 4.4% and imports by 2.2%. The cut in government consumption in this experiment amounted to DH 2,085 million. However, because tax receipts go down with the drop in economic activity, the current deficit only improves by DH 1,504 million and the total deficit by DH 1,538 million. There is an improvement in the balance of payments of DH 791 million.

Simulation 3: Increase in commodity taxes by 10%

142. An increase of all the indirect taxes by 10% in the average rate leads to a fall of GDP of about 2.3%. Private consumption decreases by 3.5%, exports by 1.6%, imports by 2% and private investment by 0.3%. The recessionary effect affects mainly industrial products, but it also spreads to high income elastic agricultural goods. The receipts of the value added tax on industry increase by DH 169 million, import taxes by DH 683 million and other indirect taxes by DH 648 million. Total tax receipts increase by DH 1,390 million, which is short of the total increase in indirect taxes, due to some shortfall in direct tax revenues. The current deficit immproves by DH 1,282 million and the balance of payments deficit by DH 560 million. Total employment decreases by 1.1%.

Simulation 4: Increase in corporate taxes

143. Two simulations were carried out: with enterprise investment fixed and with a decrease of 5%. Agriculture continued to be tax-exempt. The average tax rates for phosphates and petroleum, already high, were maintained. For the other industrial and services sectors, the rate of average corporate tax has been doubled and in certain cases tripled. However, the new rates are still very far from the statutory limit of 28%.

144. In the first simulation, GDP falls by 2%. The major fall in production is in the industrial sectors were tax rates are increased most. Some exceptions: the protected sector does not decrease as much and production falls in agricultural sectors due to the fall in aggregate expenditure. Direct taxes increase by DH 2,081 million and the overall government deficit improves by DH 1,560 million. The balance of payments improves by DH 590 million.

145. In the second simulation, enterprise investment was further reduced by 5% to account for the depressive effect that the increase in corporate tax rates could have in the short-run. In this case GDP falls by 3.1% (1.1% more than in the previous case). The improvement in the balance of payments is now higher: DH 1,028 million, but the budget deficit improves less, due to a shortfall in receipts. However, dynamic general equilibrium models built for other cases show that over time the efficiency effects of equalizing tax rates across sectors is substantial. This result is obtained due to the reallocation of capital.

Simulation 5: Increase in commodity taxes by 10% and increase in public investment by 5%.

146. Part of the recessionary effect could be counteracted by an increase in public investment. If at the same time that indirect taxes are cut by 10% public investment is increased by 5%, GDP would now fall by 2.1%, while total

investment increases by 0.4%. Naturally, the total government deficit would be about DH 126 million short of the improvement in the last simulation and the balance of payments about DH 76 million. Employment would now decrease by 1%.

Sectoral Behavior

147. The cut in government investment affects mainly construction activity. As a result, the "Protected Sector" has the largest drop in production. In view of its price rigidity, due to the mark-up formulation, that fall does not translate into a decrease in the price level. On the contrary, the reduction in supply for the flex-price sectors causes price increases (triggered mainly by intermediate goods and agricutural exportrs), which increase the "prime-costs" of the mark-up sectors. The reduction in government consumption affects, in the first phase, the income of low (6%) and middle (46%) urban classes. As a result, production falls in industrial wage goods (food and industrial exports) and other agricultural goods. The high intermediate demand linkages (input-output connections) between other agricultural products and industrial exports even leads to a fall in exports of this last group, as supply is curtailed. For both sectors, the flex-price formulation leads to price increases. The high sensitivity of the prices in both of these sectors, with a possible over-reaction by the "other agricultural products", is once more evident when commodity tax rates are increased 10% accross the board. It is interesting to note that despite a certain progressivity in the indirect tax system, due to exemption of basic foodstuffs, the impact of an uniform tax increase is regressive for urban households.

4.2 Empirical Effects of Devaluation

148. The primary impact or first round effects of a devaluation in the two-sector model of an open economy is to increase the prices of tradables relative to nontradables. The relative price effect would lead to an increase in the domestic supply and a reduction in the domestic demand of tradables, causing a decrease in imports and an increase in exports. The nontradables sector experiences an increase in demand and a decrease in supply. In the second round effects, this excess demand for nontradables leads to a increase in its price and thus reverses some of the first round effects. On the other hand, the increase in aggregate demand generated by the surplus in the trade balance[1] will lead to an increase in imports and decrease in exports, unless there is sterilization of reserves,[2] by reducing the global credit limits and/or increasing interest rates in the economy. The relative strength of these effects would determine the total outcome. However, in any reasonable trade model with stability and some degree of flexibility in prices, there is a clear improvement in the balance of payments. What is generally put in

---

1/ Equivalent to a reduction in the external trade deficit. See W. Corden, Inflation, Exchange Rates and the World Economy, U. Chicago Press, 1981.
2/ The fundamental role played by the "sterilization" process using monetary policy is clearly demonstrated in A. Mateus, "Macroeconometric Model for Stabilization Policies: The Case of Morocco", IARD, 1985.

Table 4.3: SUMMARY OF STATIC SIMULATIONS

	BASE	Devaluation	Nominal Wage increase	Oil price Shock Reversal	Phosphate Price shock
GDP at constant prices	132591.0	1.013	0.976	1.046	1.001
Price	1.000	1.027	1.033	1.000	1.008
Cereals	1.000	0.959	0.965	0.999	0.999
Agricult Exports	1.000	1.125	0.981	1.002	1.000
Sugar	1.000	1.000	1.000	1.000	1.000
Agricult Others	1.000	0.886	1.023	0.755	0.992
Phosphates	1.000	1.049	1.045	0.958	1.000
Industr Exports	1.000	1.007	1.021	0.938	0.998
Food industries	1.000	1.000	1.000	1.000	1.000
Ind Substit Others	1.000	1.045	1.034	0.994	1.000
Inter capital goods	1.000	1.057	1.039	0.992	1.000
Protected sector	1.000	1.056	1.034	0.996	1.001
Petroleum	1.000	1.104	0.997	1.000	1.000
Volume					
Cereals	13264.7	1.012	1.000	1.007	1.000
Agricult Exports	6582.7	0.980	1.002	1.035	1.001
Sugar	603.6	1.000	1.000	1.000	1.000
Agricult Others	15976.4	1.059	0.984	1.118	1.003
Phosphates	8439.8	1.008	0.989	1.009	1.000
Industr Exports	19320.9	1.058	0.978	1.085	1.003
Food industries	8866.7	1.024	1.005	1.037	1.001
Ind Substit Others	16959.2	1.044	0.961	1.050	1.001
Inter capital goods	24593.6	1.024	0.965	1.030	1.000
Protected sector	85538.9	1.004	0.982	1.040	1.001
Petroleum	14565.7	0.991	0.990	1.072	1.001
Household Consumption	89870.3	0.997	0.993	1.073	1.002
Price	1.000	1.035	1.017	0.964	0.999
Volume					
Agr households	26079.6	0.978	0.973	1.020	1.001
Urban low	43732.9	1.007	1.002	1.100	1.003
Urban middle	16731.3	1.001	0.997	1.073	1.002
Urban upper	3326.6	0.991	0.998	1.129	1.007
Investment	28427.3	0.994	0.994	1.006	1.000
Exports	26494.9	1.055	0.973	1.026	1.000
Price	1.000	1.076	1.011	0.990	1.043
Volume					
Inter capital goods	5411.0	1.106	0.910	1.019	0.999
Agriculture	1977.0	1.000	1.000	1.000	1.000
Industrial exp	4013.0	1.222	0.944	1.144	1.004
Others	9370.9	1.000	1.000	1.000	1.000
Phosphate minerals	5723.0	1.000	1.000	1.000	1.000
Imports	39051.7	0.982	0.996	1.039	1.001
Price	1.000	1.100	1.000	0.887	1.000
Volume					
Cereals	2799.0	1.000	1.000	1.000	1.000
Inter capital goods	17222.0	0.998	0.985	1.030	1.001
Others	3800.7	0.956	1.000	1.010	1.000
Oil	10673.0	0.990	0.989	1.076	1.001
Consumer ind	4557.0	0.913	1.051	1.035	1.002
Government					
Revenues	27783.5	29859.7	27862.5	28745.1	28593.4
Current expend	36118	36140.5	36102.9	36156.7	36119.4
Capital expend	3837.0	4049.2	3960.6	3804.9	3838.8
Deficit global	-10041.5	-8177.5	-10086	-9047.7	-9233.4
Balance payments					
Trade deficit	-12556.8	-12100.6	-12838.8	-9094.9	-11440.6
Current deficit	-6806.7	-4891.6	-7105.3	-3647.8	-5741.2
Terms of trade	1.000	0.978	1.011	1.116	1.043
Total employment	43022.9	1.003	0.958	1.026	1.001

question is the overall impact on economic activity: is a devaluation expansionary or recessionary? The larger the slack in capacity of production, the more elastic is the demand for exports - the usual small country assumption - and the higher is substitutability in consumption between imports and domestic production, the more will GDP grow. Finally, the real balance effect could also be a recessionary effect, but with the low degree of monetarization of a developing country, this effect seems less important.

Simulations 6: Devaluation of 10%

149.   This simulation assumes a 10% devaluation, without nominal wage adjustment. It is also assumed that there is no adjustment in the nominal figures of the government budget. Thus government consumption goes down in real terms. Exports increase by 5.5% and imports decrease by 1.8%. Tourism receipts increase by 5.1% real terms and emigrant's remittances by 2.2% in real terms. Thus, the improvement in the balance of payments is about DH 1,915 million or about 200 million dollars. We assume that devaluation has no impact on phosphate exports and that quotas are effective for agricultural exports in EEC. All the impact comes from industrial exports that rise between 10 and 20%. However, if there is some over-estimation of exports of industrial goods, that might be compensated by the fact that quotas on agricultural exports are not binding. As would be expected, industrial tradables are the sectors having the largest expansion of production, and nontradables have either a stagnation or small contraction in production. GDP increases by 1.3%. This means that a nominal devaluation of 10% translates into a real devaluation of 6.8%. The government deficit improves by DH 1,863 million, since there is a large increase in phosphate revenues (DH 2.8 million), consumer subsidies are maintained as well as other expenditures at the same level in nominal terms. There is no perceptible impact on overall employment.

150.   In the sectoral effects, it is the exports of "industrial exports" and "intermediate capital goods" that increase, since the others are exogenous, and were kept fixed in real terms. Thus, our simulation represents a clear underestimation of the effects of devaluation for those sectors. As a consequence of that behavior, it is the output of those two sectors, plus the complementary good: "agriculture: others" that experience the largest increase. The flex-price nature of most of the tradeables feeds in the "prime costs" of the nontradeables, leading to an increase of 5.6 points in the rices of the "protected sector". The nature of the formulation of the computable general equilibrium model that combines the "Armingtonian assumption" with a downward sloping demand curve for exports leads to a "terms of trade" loss, that in this case is about 2.2 points, which is relatively large.

151.   If the devaluation is combined with an increase of 3% in nominal wages and maintaining real government consumption, then GDP remains constant, exports increase now by only 2%, and imports decrease by 1.8%. There is still a substantial increase in industrial exports but the increase in aggregated demand reduces exports of nontradables and quasi-nontradables. There is no change in real wages. The balance of payments improves now by only half of the previous case.

152.   The problem of the _impact of a devaluation on the budget_ is of major concern in the adjustment process. Would a devaluation lead to an improvement or deterioration in the budget? Over the short-term, it is possible that in a highly indebted country with administratively fixed prices of some basic goods, the impact be negative. The additional payments in domestic currency for interest as well as the increased subsidies might be larger than the increase in revenues due to tariffs and commodity taxes. In Morocco, another important source of additional revenue are the phosphate sector profits. But over the medium-term, as exports and general activity pricks-up, tax revenues increase, and the sign might be reversed. This would most likely be the case if there is a complete "pass-through" of the additional import costs in administered prices. The previous simulation shows a significant improvement in the government deficit after the devaluation (from DH10 billion to DH8.2 billion), but we have assumed a fixed rate of subsidy (negative tax rate). An alternative formulation of the model fixes consumer prices of basic foodstuffs and computes subsidies as a difference between those and producer prices. As table 4.4 shows, the increase in consumer subsidies amounts to DH275 million for a 5% devaluation, and the increase in interest payments to DH375 million. However, the increase in tax revenue of DH1,028 million, largely outweights the increase in expenditure. Notice that direct taxes paid by the phosphate sector are included in "direct taxes". Despite an increase in capital expenditures of DH125 million, the total deficit only deteriorates by DH552 million.[1/]

Table 4.4:   IMPACT ON THE BUDGET OF A 5% DEVALUATION

	BASE	SIMULATED	DIFFERENCE
Total Current Receipts	29,850	31,177	+1,327
Taxes	23,277	24,305	+1,028
Direct Taxes	6,586	6,873	+287
Domestic Indirect	7,462	7,781	+319
Import Taxes	9,229	9,652	+423
Phosphate Revenues	1,740	1,857	+117
Other Revenues	6,573	6,872	+299
Total Current Expenditures	36,055	36,705	+650
Public Consumption	20,850	20,850	+0
Interest Payments	7,490	7,865	+375
Consumption Subsidies*	2,067	2,342	+275
Enterprise Subsidies	4,698	4,698	+0
Household Transfers	950	950	+0
Current Deficit	-6,205	-5,528	-677
Capital Expenses less Rec.	3,837	3,962	+125
Total Deficit	-10,042	-9,490	-552

*   Less taxes on the same goods.

[1/] One asumption made was that petroleum prices would be adjusted upwardly according to the increase in import prices.

4.3 Empirical Effects of Wage Policies

150. The general equilibrium effects of a nominal wage rate increase across the board in the formal sector would be repercuted, through the mark-up, one-to-one, to the domestic price of the sectors protected from international competition. However, for those sectors subject to competition with imports, output prices would increase proportionally to the trade elasticity. For sectors with high trade elasticity the nominal wage increase would have to be reflected in compressed profits and decreased supply. Decreased supply would decrease exports and increase imports of tradables. There is also an aggregated demand effect. The increase in wages leads to an increase in income that increases consumption and leads to an increase of demand for both nontradables and tradables. The effect on nontradables would be translated into increased supply, and the effect on tradables into increased imports and/or decreased exports. At the same time that there will be some pressure on domestic price increases.

Simulation 7:   Nominal Wage Increase (10%)

151. This simulation only gives an impulse of 10% on wages in the formal sector, including public administration. In the traditional aggregate demand-aggregate supply model, this is a supply stock that would shift the supply curve to the left and increase prices. This is exactly the outcome, GDP falls by -1.3%, while prices increase by 3.1%. The largest increases in prices are in the protected sectors (particularly administration) and in intermediate and capital goods industries. These last two are also the sectors were the drop in production is most pronounced. Employment in the urban formal sector drops by about 2.8%. The loss in competitiveness leads to a fall in exports of 2.7%, and imports of industrial consumer goods increase by 6.3%. The existence of fixed import quotas in cereals and food industries puts a cap on imports of these sectors. The government deficit deteriorates by about DH 200 million and the external deficit by DH 570 million.

4.4 External Shocks

152. Along with other less developed countries, Morocco suffered external shocks of considerable magnitude in the last decade. In the 1973-78 period, there was the quadrupling of oil prices in 1973-74[1] and the world recession of 1974-75, followed by a relatively slow recovery. The world price of phosphates increased 4.5 times in 1974 relatively to 1973, but in 1976 it had fallen 33% below 1974. However, the export price increase of phosphates largely compensated the oil price increase in 1974/75.

153. In 1979/80, Morocco suffered a second oil shock, with the doubling of oil prices. To this shock should be added the persistent recession in the industrialized world from 1980 to 1983. In 1982-85, another important shock was the sharp increase in marginal external borrowing costs due to the increase in world real interest rates and the appreciation of the dollar.

---

[1] Energy imports increased from 9% of total goods imports in 1972 to 41.4% in 1978.

154.   It is estimated that during the 1973-78 period, there was a reduction of about .9% in GDP due to terms of trade effects and also about 1.5% due to the recession in external markets. In the 1979-84 period, the terms of trade reduced GDP permanently about 3.5%, while increased recession and protectionism in external markets had an impact of about 1 to 2 percentage points of GDP. The interest rate shock amonted to about 2.7% of GDP. Of this total, 55% due to harder terms in additional borrowing and 45% due to increased interest rates on past borrowing. Thus, in contrast to a negligible total external shock in the 1973-78 period, in the recent period (1979-84) external shocks accounted for a permanent reduction of about 7.2% in GDP.

155.   An external shock in the form of an increase in the price of an intermediate good (e.g. oil) shifts the aggregate supply curve to the left causing a stagflation[1]: decrease in output and increase in prices, equivalent tonegative "technical progress". The stagflationary effect would be compounded if there is rigidity in wages or in the prices of nontradables. The increase in energy prices will reduce profitability in the energy intensive sectors. On the other hand, the loss in terms of trade will increase the deficit in the balance of payments. The macroeconomic adjustment in terms of monetary restraint and fiscal austerity can then improve the deficit. Once again, the level of contraction necessary depends crucially on the downward adjustment of real wages. Finally, it should be underscored that a permanent increase in energy prices would lead to a permanent reduction in income or wealth of the economy. The reverse effects would appear if there is a decrease in oil prices.

Simulation 8:   Oil price decrease (40%)

156.   This simulation assumes a drop of about 40% in oil prices.[2] It is assumed that this increase is fully transmitted to the domestic economy. As a consequence, there is an improvement of 11.6% in the terms of trade. There is a reduction of 3.6 percentage points in domestic inflation in terms of consumer prices, and of 2.8 percentage points in producer prices. The cut in the import bill of oil amounts to DH 3,780 million. Since GDP increases by 4.6% due to the shock in reverse, total imports increase by 3.9% in volume. It is interesting that oil imports in volume increase by 7.6%. At the same time, the decrease in domestic prices—with the assumption of all other world prices constant—leads to an improvement in competitiveness and total exports increase by 2.6% in volume. The current account of the balance of payments improves by DH 3,160 million. The global government deficit improves by about DH 994 million. The sectors experiencing the largest increase are the oil-intensive industries such as industrial exports, transport (protected), intermediate goods and the ones linked to these by inter-industry flows like construction and agriculture-others.

157.   The same experiment could be performed for an oil price increase. The previous shock would be equivalent to an increase of about 66.7% in the price of oil, with all the signs reversed.

1/ The macroeconomic effects of these external shocks have been extensively analysed by M. Bruno and J. Sachs, Economics of Worldwide Stagflation, Harvard V.P., 1985.

2/ In 1986, as an average, oil prices are expected to decrease to 16 dollars a barrel from 26 dollars in 1985.

158.   Presently the oil price decline is not being transfered to the domestic economy, but a countervailing tariff is being used. The expansionary effects on the domestic economy are cancelled, except for the government budget, that now improves by DH 4,044 million if all the reduction in the cost of oil is transfered to the Treasury. The balance of payments improves now more than in the previous case in the short-term (DH 3,810 million in this case), largely because GDP does not increase and imports do not rise consequently. However, in the medium-term, the distortions introduced by the tariff and the reduction in competitiveness in exports would lead sooner or later to a lesser improvement in the balance of payments.

Simulation 9:   Phosphate rock price increase (20%)

159.   The Moroccan economy has been subject to frequent positive and negative phosphate price shocks. A pure phosphate price increase that is not followed up by increase in government current or capital expenditures has almost no impact on GDP, imports or exports (in real terms). The major impact is on the balance of payments and on the budget. Additional export revenues amount to DH 1,444 million. The current deficit of the balance of payments improves by DH 1,066 million. The government collects about DH 810 million of additional revenue, which is the amount of the global Treasury deficit improvement.

CHAPTER V

DIFFERENT MIXTURES WITHIN POLICY PACKAGES

160.   In this chapter, we are going to study the impact on the balance of payments, GDP, government deficit, inflation and employment of different stabilization packages. The typical stabilization package comprises a cut in government expenditures (capital or current), increase in tax rates or in prices charged by public enterprises and devaluation. Another essential element of the package is a restrictive monetary policy, effected through global credit limits and, when appropriate, increase in interest rates. Since the model is a "real model", the monetary mechanisms are explicitly dealt with elsewhere [1]. The first two sections address the problem of different mixtures of measures. The first package is the most traditional stabilization package applied in Morocco, relying mainly in a cut on public investment expenditures. The second one, relies more on devaluation.

5.1 The Traditional Stabilization Package

161.   This package has been chosen by Morocco several times in the course of the last two decades when problems of the balance of payments arose. The central elements are a cut (or delay in financing) in public investment and a tightening of quantitative restrictions, increase in tariffs or increased rationing of foreign exchange allocations. When the country has to enter into a stand-by arrangement, this policy is followed up by a limited devaluation. It is generally a matter of controversy how much softening of the rationing in imports actually takes place in this follow-up, in view of the difficulty of monitoring such policies.

162.   In the medium-run, these policies have serious effects on efficiency of the economy. They increase the rate of protection in the economy and, as a consequence, promote the substitution of inefficient products and the expansion of production in sectors with low economic profitability. At the same time, the increase in tariffs and the restrictions on imports or access to foreign exchange will either increase costs or restrict access to inputs by exporters. Finally, the change in relative prices due to the overvaluation will lead to a flow of resources from the rest of the economy towards nontradables.

163.   This alternative is illustrated in Diagrams 5.1.A and 5.1.B in the context of an economy with the "Amingtonian" assumption on imports. P* are international prices and P_D, domestic prices. An increase in tariffs and QR's leads to an increase in international prices relative to nontradeables. At the same time, the cut in government investment leads to a fall in production and aggregate demand. The equilibrium point moves from A_0 to A'_1 in Diagram 5.1.A. Since the relative prices in the import

---

[1] For a monetary approach to the balance of payments model, see the study of A. Mateus "A Macroeconomic Model for Stabilization Policies: the case of Morocco", 1985.

Diagram 5.1.A

Inward-Oriented Stabilization Package

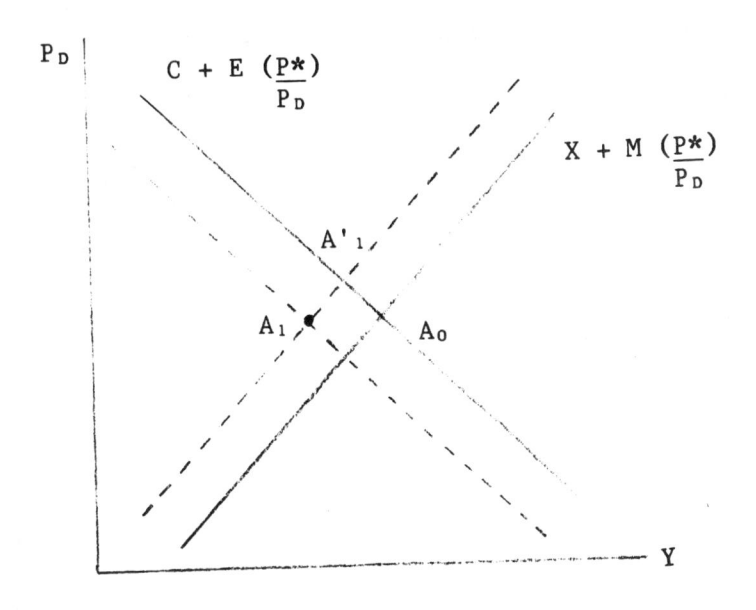

Diagram 5.1.B

Outward-Oriented Stabilization Package

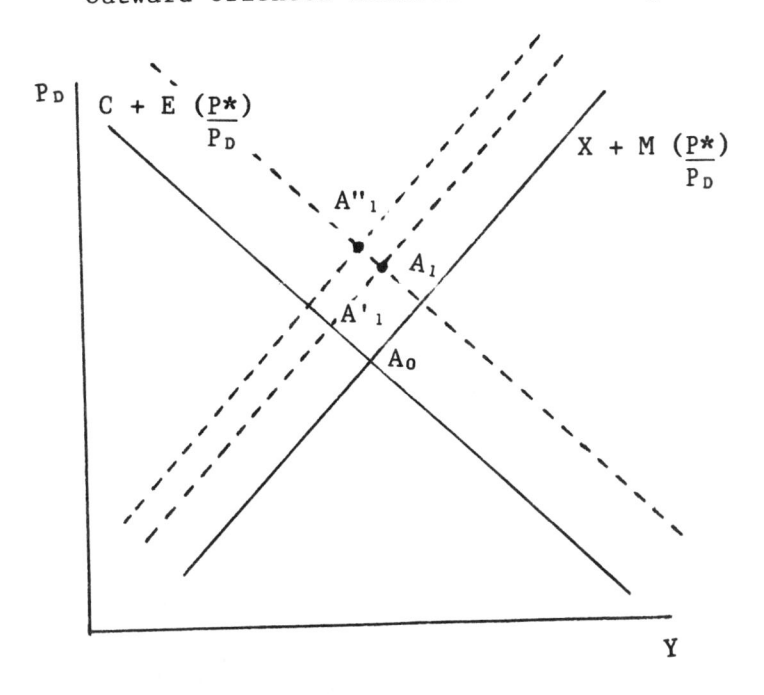

substitute sectors go up, there is a diversion of resources away from the export sectors aggravated by the increase in costs of inputs due to increase in protection, and the equilibrium point moves to A_1, with lower income than in A_0.

Simulation 10: Increase in import taxes (10%), tightening of import quotas (30%), cut in government comsumption (5%), cut in government investment (20%).

164. As a result of the package, total imports decrease by 4.5%, and exports decrease by 0.3%. The fall in exports is not even more pronounced due to the fact that wages fall slightly in real terms, and there is a cut in domestic demand for the export sectors. GDP decreases by 1.5%. The balance of payments improves by DH 1,745 million: DH 755 million due to the cut in government expenditures and DH 990 million due to trade restrictions. The increase in tariffs brings in about DH 839 million to the Treasury. Combined with the cut in expenditures it improves by about DH 2,228 million the overall budget. This policy adds only half of a percent to the inflation rate. Employment falls by 3.6% in the formal sector.

5.2. An Outward-Oriented Package

165. Instead of putting the burden of adjustment in expenditure reducing, a different policy package has been proposed that emphasizes expenditure switching. This package uses devaluation instead of import controls or tariffs to bring about most of the improvement in the balance of payments. The success of devaluation depends on several important factors like (i) degree of capacity utilization; (ii) downward flexibility of wages and prices in the tradables sectors. Obviously, large unused capacity in the tradeables sectors would improve exports and reduce imports in the first round effects. Unused capacity in the protected sectors and downward adjustment of real wages as well as prices in the non tradable sectors would also magnify the favorable effects. Finally, devaluation has always to be used in conjunction with some cut in aggregate demand to stabilize the effect of the increase in international reserves. Another favorable effect of a devaluation is the probable increase in employment in the economy. In the outward-oriented policy, Diagram 5.1.B, there is also an increase in import prices, and reduction in government expenditure, leading to a virtual fall in income represented by A'_1. But, since exports become more profitable, external demand expands, cancelling part of the negative effect on income, reaching A''_1. As production in the export sectors picks-up, it can accelerate the recovery (the equilibrium point moves from A''_1 to A_1), leading to an overall increase in income.

Simulation 11: Cut in government consumption (5%), cut in government investment (10%), and devaluation (10%).

166. In this simulation, we had as a target to obtain approximately the same cut in GDP and employment as in the previous simulation. Now we use a combination of cuts in government expenditure and devaluation substitutes for trade restrictions and increase in tariffs of the previous simulation. At the same time, the reduction in public investment was lower than in the previous package. By using a 10% devaluation and a cut of 10% in public investment instead of the 20% in the previous case, GDP only decreases by 1.2% and

employment by 2.4%. In both cases less than in simulation 10. However, now the deficit of the balance of payments improves by DH 2,485, while in the previous case the improvement was DH 1,745 million. Exports increase now by 5%, against a fall in the previous case, while imports decrease now about one percentage point less than in the previous case. The global government deficit in this simulation improves by DH 2,894 million, against DH 2,229 in the inward-oriented policy. Only the inflation rate deteriorates relatively to the previous scenario: from 0.5 to 3.8 percentage points.

167. One of the compromises frequently done is to cut more public investment and have a lower devaluation. In an alternative simulation, public investment was cut by 25% against 10% in the previous case, while devaluation was now 5% against 10% in the previous case. The result is a larger drop in GDP (2.4%) and employment (2.9%). It is true that about 1.4 percentage points are gained in terms of inflation, but the reduction in the external deficit is now DH 745 million short of the previous case, and the government deficit DH 555 million. Even the so-called "social impact" cannot be used as a justification for this last alternative, since both consumption and income of the lower income classes drop more in this case than in the previous one.

5.3 Trade-offs and Constraints

168. The trade-offs and conflicts among the common targets in economic policy: growth reduction in external deficit and reduction in inflation are brought out in Table 7.1. The table presents the static multipliers and elasticities for the different policy instruments with the simulations previously made. The most important conclusions are:

- o devaluation is the only instrument that has a positive affect on GDP and reduces the external deficit simultaneously. This compatibility of objectives is greater the more unused capacity there is in the initial situation and the less is the downward rigidity of factor prices;

- o contraction (expansion) of government investment is more effective in reducing (increasing) external deficit, and decreases (increases) GDP and employment less than government changes in consumption;

- o for the same reduction in the global government deficit, a cut in government consumption is more effective in improving the external deficit than an increase in commodity taxes;[1]

- o but for the same reduction is the government deficit, a cut in government consumption is more recessionary than an increase in commodity taxes.[2]

---

[1] The ratios are .51 and .44, respectively.

[2] The ratios are 3.37 and 2.13, respectively.

PART III: EMPIRICAL ANALYSIS OF STRUCTURAL ADJUSTMENT POLICIES

CHAPTER VI

EMPIRICAL EFFECTS OF STRUCTURAL ADJUSTMENT POLICIES

169. Structural adjustment policies have been carried with the objective of changing the structure of the economy with a medium-term horizon. The areas where economic policy in Morocco has been concentrated are:

(i) <u>trade liberalization</u>, reduction in the maximum level of tariffs, across-the-board cuts in tariffs, decreases in quantitative restrictions on imports, and domestic price liberalization;

(ii) <u>tax reform</u>: overhaul of commodity taxation by full implementation of a value added tax; elimination of consumer subsidies on basic foods; elimination of investment and sectoral codes giving special concessions and exemptions; cuts in import taxes;

(iii) <u>agricultural prices and incentives reform</u>, which has several ingredients common to trade liberalization, transformation of quotas into tariffs, price liberalization, elimination of input subsidies, and liberalization of crop systems in irrigated areas.

170. Other areas of reform like public enterprise, education, and financial sectors are more difficult to model in the present context and are consequently left out of the study.

6.1 Trade Liberalization

171. The trade regime in Morocco is characterized by: (i) quantitative restrictions that have pervaded most of the structure of imports under the so called lists B and C (staple imports are subject to the control of import monopolies); (ii) a system of custom duties that clusters around 40 to 100% with some important exemptions, and imports for exports under special trade regimes, agricultural imports and most of capital goods;
(iii) across-the-board import taxes, a special import tax, and a stamp duty. Trade restrictions on exports include the state monopoly on phosphates and derivatives, a marketing board on agricultural exports and until recently an across-the-board statistical tax on exports.[1]

172. Since 1967, all imports have been classified in three groups. Commodities included in the first list (list A) can be freely imported; commodities included in list B are subject to import licensing; and list C commodities cannot be imported except under derogatory conditions. Table 6.2 reports the share of total imports in list B, both at an aggregate level and for disaggregated functional categories. This share steadily increased after

---

[1] For a detailed discussion of the trade regime see Morocco: Industrial Incentives and Export Promotion, IBRD, 1983.

Table 6.1: SUMMARY OF STATIC SIMULATIONS

	BASE	Stabilization Policy Inward-Orient	Stabilization Policy Outward-Orient	Trade Liberalization	Tax Reform	Agricult Sector Reform	Trade Liberalizati with Compensatory Devaluation
GDP at constant prices	132591.0	0.985	1.018	0.984	0.894	1.005	1.002
Price	1.000	1.005	0.999	0.996	1.063	1.006	1.005
Cereals	1.000	1.004	0.992	1.009	0.964	0.926	0.985
Agricult Exports	1.000	1.001	0.992	1.010	1.012	0.999	1.069
Sugar	1.000	1.000	1.000	1.000	1.000	1.000	1.000
Agricult Others	1.000	1.015	0.872	1.127	1.873	1.042	0.989
Phosphates	1.000	1.003	1.007	0.990	1.000	1.001	1.015
Industr Exports	1.000	1.003	0.970	1.025	1.228	1.013	1.010
Food industries	1.000	1.000	1.000	1.000	1.000	1.000	1.000
Ind Substit Others	1.000	1.001	1.006	0.989	1.020	1.004	1.012
Inter capital goods	1.000	1.004	1.013	0.983	0.975	1.001	1.014
Protected sector	1.000	0.999	1.013	0.983	0.979	1.001	1.016
Petroleum	1.000	1.000	0.999	1.001	1.002	1.000	1.053
Volume							
Cereals	13264.7	1.064	1.066	0.955	0.982	1.108	0.963
Agricult Exports	6582.7	0.990	1.011	0.988	0.902	1.001	0.986
Sugar	603.6	1.000	1.000	1.000	1.000	1.000	1.000
Agricult Others	15976.4	0.987	1.046	0.948	0.791	0.989	1.015
Phosphates	8439.8	0.996	0.999	0.997	0.987	1.001	1.007
Industr Exports	19320.9	0.988	1.032	0.964	0.782	0.988	1.021
Food industries	8866.7	1.000	1.027	0.980	0.889	0.990	1.000
Ind Substit Others	16959.2	0.995	1.021	0.974	0.845	0.997	1.007
Inter capital goods	24593.6	0.987	0.998	0.993	0.958	1.003	1.022
Protected sector	85538.9	0.982	1.008	0.993	0.913	1.004	1.003
Petroleum	14565.7	0.985	1.003	0.996	0.945	1.006	0.998
Household Consumption	89870.3	0.981	1.014	0.989	0.845	0.998	1.001
Price	1.000	1.005	0.995	1.000	1.081	1.007	1.012
Volume							
Agr households	26079.6	1.010	1.006	1.000	0.944	1.000	0.990
Urban low	43732.9	0.967	1.020	0.983	0.799	0.997	1.006
Urban middle	16731.3	0.972	1.013	0.990	0.816	0.999	1.004
Urban upper	3326.6	0.982	1.013	0.993	0.838	0.997	1.001
Investment	28427.3	0.972	0.999	1.002	0.989	1.001	0.999
Exports	26494.9	0.997	1.003	1.003	0.960	0.995	1.034
Price	1.000	1.001	0.999	0.999	1.014	1.002	1.036
Volume							
Inter capital goods	5411.0	0.992	0.969	1.044	1.063	0.998	1.090
Agriculture	1977.0	1.000	1.000	1.000	1.000	1.000	1.000
Industrial exp	4013.0	0.994	1.058	0.957	0.652	0.972	1.100
Others	9370.9	1.000	1.000	1.000	1.000	1.000	1.000
Phosphate minerals	5723.0	1.000	1.000	1.000	1.000	1.000	1.000
Imports	39051.7	0.955	0.973	1.036	0.959	0.974	1.018
Price	1.000	1.000	1.000	1.000	1.000	1.000	1.050
Volume							
Cereals	2799.0	0.700	0.700	1.200	1.000	0.577	1.200
Inter capital goods	17222.0	0.983	1.003	1.012	0.939	1.004	1.003
Others	3800.7	0.973	0.978	1.108	1.025	1.004	1.003
Oil	10673.0	0.984	1.003	0.996	0.942	1.006	0.998
Consumer ind	4557.0	0.927	0.949	1.062	0.998	1.006	1.028
Government							
Revenues	27783.5	28203	28798.4	26420	32443.6	28920.7	27506
Current expend	36118	35076.9	36136.8	36101.6	34981.1	35818.3	36120.5
Capital expend	3837.0	3070.2	3879.5	3778.8	3858.1	3844.7	3897.9
Deficit global	-10041.5	-7812.7	-9069.1	-11346.7	-5402.5	-9152.1	-10379.9
Balance payments							
Trade deficit	-12556.8	-10859.3	-11449.5	-13934.1	-11673.3	-11618.4	-13387.4
Current deficit	-6806.7	-5062	-5730.8	-8147.2	-5490.4	-5878.5	-6903.6
Terms of trade	1.000	1.001	0.999	0.999	1.014	1.002	0.987
Total employment	43022.9	0.975	1.006	0.994	0.954	1.004	1.002

Table 6.2: TRADE REGIME: QUANTITATIVE RESTRICTIONS
AND ACROSS-THE-BOARD IMPORT TAXES

	Share of Imports Under QR's					
	Agricultural Goods	Semi-Finished Products	Investment Goods	Consumption Goods	Special Import Tax	Stamp Duty
1967	65.3	36.4	23.8	60.7	2.5	1.0
1968	65.3	36.4	23.8	60.7	2.5	1.0
1969	65.3	36.4	23.8	60.7	2.5	1.0
1970	26.8	17.2	22.4	22.3	2.5	1.0
1971	26.8	18.5	24.8	21.8	2.5	1.0
1972	26.7	19.7	27.2	21.3	2.5	1.0
1973	52.7	17.9	28.6	37.0	2.5	4.0
1974	44.8	21.8	30.5	18.0	2.5	4.0
1975	46.2	32.0	35.8	16.5	2.5	4.0
1976	45.0	32.8	28.1	13.8	2.5	4.0
1977	58.3	41.4	22.2	22.8	8.0	4.0
1978	64.7	52.8	39.7	57.6	12.0	4.0
1979	69.7	39.1	80.6	81.3	13.5	10.0
1980	61.6	32.4	63.0	61.3	15.0	10.0
1981	64.4	34.9	61.2	61.0	15.0	10.0
1982	65.7	29.5	23.7	60.0	15.0	10.0
1983	91.8	39.1	67.6	77.3	15.0	10.0
1984	12.1	27.0	24.7	60.0	10.0	10.0

Source: Office de Change

1972 as a result of the government policy aimed at speeding up industrialization by import-substitution. It peaked twice, in 1978/79 and in 1983, when a deteriorating current account balance forced Moroccan authorities to take emergency measures to curtail imports. The special import tax and the stamp duty represent across the board import duties. The latter is a surcharge based on all other taxes. Table 6.2 reports their evolution, and both show a peak in 1979-83.

173. Quantitative restrictions have been used quite extensively by LDC's in the 1950s and 1960s as an essential instrument of the import-substitution strategy. In contrast to a tariff, quotas generate monopoly power for a single producer in the country. They create a premium that accrues to the producer (or importer) instead of the revenue of a tariff that accrues to the Treasury.[1] Bhagwati and Krueger in their NBER study do a remarkable job in analyzing the distortions arising from the elaborate and complex QR regimes they observe including excess plant capacity, failure to absorb unskilled labor into the industrial labor force, corruption and smuggling, repression of exports, and substitution of the market by the bureaucratic competition among licensees. On the other hand, the extreme inefficiencies and anomalies evident in the static allocation of resources are compounded by the dynamic inefficiencies arising from a protected sector where technical progress is not rewarded, economies of scale are not exploited, and compression of costs not incentivated. These are the main reasons why they consider the transformation of QR's into tariffs the basic ingredient of a trade liberalization package. Another important argument to require the immediate transformation of all QR's into tariffs is the difficulty in monitoring a program of reduction of protection in the economy if there is a mixture of tariffs and quotas. Simply reducing the number of items in a list of restricted exports does not tell anything to the policy maker. E.g. restrictive quotas could be eliminated on inputs and maintained on outputs competing with domestic production to increase the level of protection.

1/ Except for cereals, import licenses are never auctioned off in Morocco.

174. The next step in trade liberalization is to cut tariffs in order to decrease the average level of protection in the economy. Two methods have been used thus far. The first, the "concertina method" cuts the maximum tariff rate and imposes some minimum tariff across the board. The second method cuts tariffs across the board. Both methods have been demonstrated to be welfare improving thus far as they move the system of protection towards uniformity at an acceptable rate of effective protection across the board. As we know from the theory of optimal taxation, a uniform protective tariff is not optimal since it introduces distortions through the input-output system and the taxing of intermediate goods. However, it might be a reasonable compromise in view of the demands for protection arising from the different pressure groups. The revenue raising argument for tariffs is very difficult to maintain. Once the government has to use domestic commodity taxation to complement its resources, only commodities that flow to the untaxed sector (agriculture, services or handicrafts) should be taxed at the customs level. All the other commodities that are imported and enter into the taxed sector should be taxed at the same rate as domestic goods at the final stage, once they leave the taxed sector (e.g. when they are consumed). A full implementation of a Value Added Tax would have these characteristics.

175. In a small country economy, the optimal level of tariffs is zero, except for a product where the country has monopoly power (case of phosphates), or dumping is manifest. If there are infant industries, then the instruments to use are production subsidies. Only if there are revenue constraints, in a third-best situation, tariffs should be used.[1] This last case might be the present case of Morocco. The revenue question is dealt with in the next section, in the overall context of the tax reform.

176. <u>The macroeconomics of trade liberalization</u> is a very important and relevant subject, since Morocco is trying to liberalize at the same time that a stabilization program to redress the desequilibrium in the government budget and external account are underway.

177. The most important principle is that any trade liberalization has to be compensated in the short term by an equivalent devaluation to avoid the deterioration of the external deficit and the consequent loss in reserves.[2]

---

[1] The continuing persistance of excess demand in the foreign exchange market leads to the conclusion that there continues to be overvaluation of the exchange rate. If there are political constraints in using devaluation as a policy instrument, then the argument is frequently advanced that an across the board tariff should be used to maintain the equilibrium in the balance of payments. However, the theoretical equivalence between devaluation and tariffs only holds if there is the same level of subsidy to all exports. If these subsidies are not effectively used, then exports are penalized. It should be recognized that exemption of tariffs on inputs used in exports is already a significant step in decreasing that penalization.

[2] Using a macroeconomic model, M. Kahn and R. Zahler, "Trade and Financial Liberalization Given External Shocks and Inconsistent Domestic Policies", IMF Staff Papers, March 1985, illustrate the massive loss in international reserves and build-up of the external debt that can occur if trade and financial liberalization are conducted at the same time that inconsistant domestic policies (e.g overvalued fixed exchange rates, wage indexation or large fiscal deficits) are pursued. The real life examples of the Latin American Southern Cone are dramatic illustrations.

178. The presence of quotas complicates and lowers the effects of adjustment induced by a devaluation or monetary policies. The results[1] are that the presence of a quota magnifies, in the short run, the reduction in terms of foreign exchange of the relative price of the non-traded goods following a devaluation. In the second round, the excess demand generated in the quota constrained as well as in non traded goods markets leads to an increase in their money prices, reducing money balances by more than in the case of a tariff ridden economy. The quota constrained sector is thus equivalent to a non-traded goods sector, and the larger these sectors are relative to the tradeables, the more macroeconomic adjustment is required to eliminate an imbalance on the balance of payments. The presence of quotas also reduces the speed of adjustment to the new long-term equilibrium following devaluation and trade liberalization. Where there is a liberalization of the quota constraint, a devaluation shortens the adjustment period and can prevent unemployment when there is downward rigidity of prices.

179. Finally, in a country where the fiscal deficit is of major concern, the immediate transformation of quotas into tariffs would decrease the quota premiums or rent-seeking of the protected sectors and increase the revenues to the Treasury. If the liberalization takes the form of a cut in tariffs, this would decrease receipts to the Treasury. It would probably be partially compensated by the increase in import volumes due to cheaper imports. If a compensated devaluation is used, import prices increase and GDP expands resulting from the expansion of exports, generating additional revenues. However, the total effect is some shortfall in revenues that would have to be compensated by increase in general commodity taxation.

Simulation 12: increase in import quotas in food sectors (20%), increase in trade elasticities and cut in import taxes (15%)

180. Trade elasticities used were assumed at a minimum of 2, except for oil where we continued to assume complementary. Cuts in import taxes across-the-board were the following:

Table 6.3: IMPORT TAX RATES

	Old	New
AGREP	.169	.144
AGRP-O	.363	.309
PHOSPH	.264	.244
PETROL	.170	.145
INDEXP	.448	.381
INDS-F	.275	.234
INDS-O	.322	.274
INDIMP	.269	.229

[1] See J. Aizenman, Devaluation and Liberalization in the presence of tariff and quotas restrictions, Journal of International Economics, II (1981).

The results of trade liberalization are an increase in imports of 3.6% and in exports of .3%. This last result is due to a slight increase in industrial exports. GDP falls by 1.6% in volume and the GDP deflator by .4%. Total employment falls by 0.6%. The government deficit increases by DH 1,305 million mainly due to the shortfall in import taxes (DH 1,125 million). Finally the balance of payments deteriorates by DH 1,340 million. These results have to be interpreted as short-term efforts as production suffers mostly from increased competition of imports. Cereals and the more open industrial sectors are the ones suffereing most. Since we fixed capital at the sectoral level, welfare only increases due to labor reallocation. Another factor that contributes to the decrease in GDP is the low elasticity in the transformation curve caused by the fixed coefficients in intermediate demand.

6.2 Tax Reform

181. While the stabilization aspects of tax reform have been dealt with in the previous two chapters, this section concentrates on the resource allocation, efficiency, and income distribution aspects of the tax system. The purposes of the tax reform in Morocco are to: (i) increase the level of revenues to the Treasury and increase the "buoyancy ratio" of the tax system; (ii) harmonize the tax system with the other objectives of improving the efficiency of resource allocation and in particular with trade liberalization; and (iii) ensure that the "tax burden" is shared in an equitable way across the population groups.

182. The main components of the tax reform package are:

(i) harmonization of commodity taxation; full implementation of the VAT, extension to small and medium-sized firms, harmonization of the tax rates and modernization of the excise tax system. In the case of basic food staples, the priority is to eliminate food subsidies and use direct food aid;

(ii) elimination of all investment and sectoral tax codes, except the export code - in this case reduction of concessions to half of the corporate tax. Transformation of the system of investment incentives into savings incentives;

(iii) elimination of the distortions in profit taxation by proceeding in the following steps: (a) elimination of investment codes; (b) integration of the corporate and personal income taxes; and (c) gradual transformation of the personal income tax into expenditure tax, (the corporate tax rate could be decreased from 50% to 40% as a compensatory measure);

(iv) gradual reduction of the level of effective protection;

(v) introduction of a land tax and import taxes on inputs to agriculture in order to avoid the present almost nil contribution of the sector to revenues; and

(vi) modernization of the income tax system with improved administration, more uniform treatment of deductions and tax credits, and a cut in the higher marginal tax rates.

183. Table 6.4 summarizes the changes in tax rates proposed. Average income tax rates are assumed to remain constant. The statutory rates are already quite high. Whatever proposed reduction in the higher marginal tax rates is finally implemented, it is compensated by improved administration and possible repeal of certain allowances and credits in the system. The repeal of the investment codes and sectoral codes would generate a significant increase in average corporate tax rates. Except for phosphates and petroleum, all the other effective tax rates vary between 1.7 and 7.3% on gross profits. It is assumed that those rates increase to 8 to 12%. The current reform of the protection system is assumed to cut 20% from the average tariff rate. All the quotas are assumed to be replaced by tariffs (cereals being one of the most important). Finally, on commodity taxation, consumer subsidies are reduced by half. The VAT and indirect taxes are increased from a band of 1 to 16.9% to an interval of 5.8 to 19%.

Simulation 15   Tax Reform

184. This package of tax reform generates an increase of DH 5,376 million in additional Treasury revenues. Combined with the decrease of DH 1,137 million in consumer subsidies generates a global improvement in the budget of DH 4,639 million, which is the estimated required improvement in the short-term to balance the structural deficit. There is an estimated short-run fall on GDP of about 10%, which raises the need to spread the tax reform over a period of 3 to 4 years in order for the efficiency gains in allocation of resources and the recovery of private investment to take place. Simultaneously, if the compensatory programs for food subsidies are implemented, about 2.5 points could be saved from the drop in GDP. The sectors most affected are agriculture-others, industrial exports and industries that are mostly import substitutes. Exports of manufactured products would also be affected. One of the possibilities to be seriously considered is maintaining the profit tax exemption (or a 50% reduction) for exporters. The balance of payments improves by about DH 1,371 million. Due to the substantial cut in food subsidies, 8 points are added to inflation. Finally, the impact on income distribution is relatively small for agricultural households but substantial for urban households: 20% reduction for lower, 18.4% for middle and 16.2% for upper income classes. Once again the need of compensatory food programs is established. The implementation of those programs would reduce the recessionary effects of the package by about two thirds.

6.3 Other Supply-Side Policies: Agricultural Sector Adjustment

185. Several policy reforms are underway in agriculture in order to improve the efficiency of the sector. The major components of the reform are: i) external trade liberalization across the sector, lifting prohibitions and other quantitative restrictions on exports and imports, and instituting a small effective protection rate across all subsectors; ii) liberalization of domestic markets in grains; iii) gradual elimination of consumer subsidies and expansion of direct food aid programs to compensate the urban poor;

Table 6.4: SUMMARY OF TAX REFORM

	BASE VALUE	BASE RATE	TAX PROPOSAL
CORPORATE TAX			
RVC-AGREXP			
RVC-AGR-CE			
RVC-PHOSPH	1012.700	.218	.218
RVC-PETROL	177.800	.168	.168
RVC-INDEXP	65.100	.017	.090
RVC-INDS-F	6.000	.073	.100
RVC-INDS-O	79.000	.028	.090
RVC-PROTEC	1219.600	.037	.080
RVC-AGRP-O	1.600	.000	.000
RVC-INDIMP	19.800	.037	.120
DIRECT TAX			
MNGAGR	564.500	.017	.017
MNGOUVR	412.900	.009	.009
MNGEMPL	1493.000	.062	.062
MNGECADR	438.000	.073	.073
ENTREPRIS	984.600	.037	.037
VALUE ADDED TAX			
EMT-PHOSPH	51.458	.058	.058
EMT-INDEXP	21.188	.011	.060
EMT-INDS-O	216.476	.083	.110
EMT-PROTEC	126.748	.010	.090
EMT-INDIMP	574.253	.169	.190
CPT-PHOSPH	269.242	.058	.058
CPT-INDEXP	42.312	.011	.060
CPT-INDS-O	232.024	.083	.110
CPT-PROTEC	322.152	.010	.090
CPT-INDIMP	866.047	.169	.190
TARIFF ON IMPORTS			
IMP-AGREXP	11.600	.169	.135
IMP-AGR-CE			.200
IMP-PHOSPH	19.000	.264	.211
IMP-PETROL	1815.600	.170	.136
IMP-INDEXP	1006.600	.448	.358
IMP-INDS-F	113.200	.275	.220
IMP-INDS-O	1336.400	.322	.258
IMP-AGRP-O	291.200	.363	.290
IMP-INDIMP	4635.800	.269	.215
INDIRECT TAX			
CMT-AGREXP	106.700	.013	.030
CMT-AGR-CE	-939.600	-.051	-.020
CMT-AGRP-S	1.300	.014	.030
CMT-PHOSPH	13.500	.005	.005
CMT-PETROL	91.700	.003	.003
CMT-INDEXP	-448.000	-.020	-.010
CMT-INDS-F	-742.400	-.077	-.050
CMT-INDS-O	2075.500	.087	.100
CMT-PROTEC	2127.500	.036	.050
CMT-AGRP-O	261.100	.014	.030
CMT-INDIMP	112.700	.002	.010
CMT-ADMINS	4.600	.000	.000
SOCIAL SECURITY TAX			
EMT-AGREXP	58.026	.055	.055
EMT-AGR-CE	69.878	.055	.055
EMT-AGRP-S	2.963	.056	.056
EMT-PHOSPH	157.904	.178	.178
EMT-PETROL	23.704	.108	.108
EMT-INDEXP	10.249	.054	.054
EMT-INDS-F	104.076	.083	.083
EMT-INDS-O	293.463	.113	.113
EMT-PROTEC	1085.084	.083	.083
EMT-AGRP-O	51.483	.055	.055
EMT-INDIMP	498.899	.147	.147
EMT-ADMINS	1448.671	.088	.088

iv) freeing crop systems in irrigated areas in order to better respond to market price signals (this would entail a drop in sugar production, a crop heavily subsidized by the goverment); and v) progressive elimination of input subsidies, specially on fertilizers and water.

186. Several components of the program: reduction of consumer subsidies and a decrease in sugar production with or without compensatory programs have been already simulated and the results reported elsewhere.[1] Assuming fixed nominal wages, the cut in food subsidies leads to a decrease in real income and would have recessionary effects, although entailing positive effects on the government deficit and balance of payments. Concern for the social costs would recommend stepping up the direct food aid and other income transfer programs that would be less distortionary. Liberalization of domestic markets of grains and of crop patterns in irrigated areas would lead to an increase in total factor productivity. The reduction in input subsidies, particularly in fertilizer, would lead to an increase in costs of production and a reduction in production of fertilizer-intensive crops. However, the change in trade regime for cereals, to the extent that would increase producer prices and correct for the negative protection observed for the most important traditonal grains, would compensate for the previous effect. Simulations with an econometric grain markets model built for Morocco, imbedding a dynamic adjustment, were reported elsewhere.[2] On balance, the measures reported above, in conjunction with more normal levels of rainfall, would increase production by about 1.4% per year.

Simulation 14: Cut in food subsidies (25%), direct income transfer (240 million), replacement of the quota by a 20% tariff.

187. Production of cereals increases by 10.8%, which pushes up GDP by 0.6%. Consumer prices increase by 0.7%. Contrary to the case where only consumer subsidies are eliminated and transfers effected, agricultural households do not experience a loss of income. The balance of payments improves by DH 928 million and the government deficit by DH 889 million.

---

[1] See Morocco: Compensatory Measures for Reducing Food Subsidies, IBRD, 1986.
[2] See IBRD, Agriculture Prices and Incentives, 1986, 3 volumes.

CHAPTER VII

STABILIZATION-CUM-STRUCTURAL ADJUSTMENT POLICIES

7.1 Fine-Tuning of Stabilization-cum-Structural Adjustment

188.   Trying to liberalize trade from a situation of large external deficit is a very difficult policy decision. In fact, trade liberalization would tend to lead to a decrease in import prices and increase in real wealth. In a flexible exchange and interest rate economy, this is translated into real appreciation of the exchange rate and increase in interest rate, a consequent deterioration of the current account and an inflow of capital. However, if inflationary expectations persist and the government tries to intervene in the exchange rate market to avoid inflation, there follows a period of outflow of capital, loss in reserves and possible collapse of the liberalization attempt. The control of external capital flows seems to play a major role in the process due to the externality involved in foreign borrowing. When an individual firm uses external borrowing, it does not take into account the effect on the creditworthiness of the country.

189.   Most of the more recently visible experiments on trade liberalization were associated with domestic financial and external capital flows liberalization.

190.   The experiments of the Southern Cone of Latin America, involving Argentina, Chile and Uruguay, have all ended in financial disaster. Although other countries like Mexico, Peru, Morocco and many others also experienced some liberalization[1], those experiments collapsed with the flare up of the debt crisis. In the case of the Southern Cone, some authors have argued that the reason for the lack of success was that domestic inflation expectations were sluggish in the short-run, so that a reduction in the rate of depreciation (politically induced, in order to stabilize prices) immediately reduced the real interest rate through its effect on the nominal rates. This change in turn stimulated spending, causing real appreciation, which was at the origin of the consequent deterioration of the current account. Others tie real appreciation to sluggishness in price adjustment in the goods markets disequilibrium. In this case, devaluation runs behind domestic inflation without ever catching it--a recipe for disaster. Others emphasize the portfolio shifts into domestic nonmoney assets and public disbelief in the official renunciation of upcoming surprise maxi-devaluations. Risk associated with domestic money assets increases and people just run for the dollar. The most important conclusions of all this literature are: i) trade liberalization in the context of free foreign capital flows is a very risky endeavor, i.e. trade liberalization must precede capital account

---

[1] In other words, there is no correlation between trade and financial liberalization attempts and external debt crisis. In most other cases, the problem was caused by government over-borrowing.

liberalization and ii) trade or financial liberalization cannot be conducted in the presence of continuous domestic disequilibrium. Of tantamount importance are fiscal deficits. In fact, most of the successful cases of liberalization have respected these principles, like the by now nearly forgotten cases of the formation of the European Community or European Free Trade Association,[1] or Korea in the 1960s.

191. Since our model is a real economy model, it does not capture the richness of the effects just described; however, the real effects need to be taken into account. First, to the extent that trade liberalization in the context of a fixed exchange rate would lead to a substantial loss in foreign exchange reserves. Second, that it needs to be made in the context of a stabilization program. To solve the first problem, when the country faces a tight foreign credit constraint, it needs to adopt a compensated devaluation. The "superiority" of a compensated devaluation, in terms of welfare, vis-a-vis a straight devaluation, is that it has less inflationary effects: the cut in prices of the importables due to the reduction in import taxes or premium of quotas more than compensates the devaluation. The second is the static, and above all, the dynamic efficiency effects of the decrease in distortions engendered by the harmonization and cut in protection. On the other hand, it might be argued, from a political economy viewpoint, that it is during times of crisis that the government has more leverage to remove privileges given to special interest group by the protection system. Returning to diagram 5.1.B, a reduction in protection would lead to a lower increase in import prices when associated with a devaluation, the aggregate supply curve would not shift as much to the left, and consequently there would be a lower recessionary impact.

192. One of the most surprising results of the CGE simulation is how important macroeconomic management of aggregate demand is to the success of the liberalization process. Suppose aggregate demand is maintained at the same level in constant terms, which would imply that when domestic prices start to fall under high export and supply elasticities, exports start immediately to rise. Then, in the short-run, before imports start to rise, it is possible to observe an improvement in the current account.

193. If the starting situation is one of large government and current account deficit, then the other instruments of fiscal policy--government expenditures and taxes--have to be used in conjunction with monetary policy in order to reduce those deficits. Yet, these policies are clearly contractionary. However, as we have indicated above in Chapter VI, it is expected that private investment and labor effort would increase in the medium-term. That is why the Government needs to pay more attention to supply side policies. Several recent studies[2] have emphasized that combining supply policies with stabilization policies would alleviate the contraction needed over the medium-term. The crucial problem is exactly the medium to long lag in supply response to reform policies. For example, in cereals

---

[1] These cases are not unilateral trade liberalization, but multilateral cases, so the push in exports due to the custom union formation might compensate in certain cases the increase in imports.

[2] See, for example M. Khan and M. Knight, Adjustment Policies in Developing Countries, IMF Occasional Paper, 1985.

markets, response of grain production to support producer price policies is relatively sluggish in the short-run (average elasticity across grains is about .4), while after three to four years the response is high (long-run elasticity reaches about 1).

Simulation 15: Import taxes cut across the board (15%), import quotas loosened (increased by 20%) and compensatory devaluation (5%).

194.   This simulation retakes the previous trade liberalization policy and computes the compensatory devaluation needed to cut the external deficit to its initial level. The cut in tariffs represents a change from an average import tax of .25 to .213. In the case of the Moroccan Special Import Tax, this represents a cut of 3.75 percentage points. Notice, however, that this reduction is compounded by the easing of import quotas, that in practice are difficult (if not impossible) to measure. In the simulation it is found that within this context a devaluation of about 5% is required. Although the devaluation closes the external gap, the government deficit deteriorates by DH 204 million due to the shortfall in revenue. Exports increase now by 3.4% (3 percentage points above the straight trade liberalization case) and imports by 1.8% (1.8 percentage points below the pure trade liberalization case). GDP increases by 0.2%[1], and the GDP deflator by only half of a percent. Total employment increases by 0.2%. These effects constitute a reversal of the pure trade liberalization case.

7.2 Social Costs of Stabilization and Adjustment

195.   There has been a recent controversy about the social costs of stabilization and adjustment[2] in developing countries. One side claims that the recent programs have substantially deteriorated the status of the poor, while the other claims that hardly any evidence can be presented to substantiate that contention. In order to identify the effects of different policy measures, a model is needed. The measurement of the impact of the stabilization packages by income group depends crucially on the institutional characteristics of the economy and the "closure-rule" assumed. Are nominal wage rates fixed in the formal sector? Do government expenditures respond to the level of activity? Is investment exogenous or determined by available savings? Apart from these aspects, the impact of adjustment on the poor depends on structural characteristics. If export production is largely raw labor intensive (e.g. in clothing and tourism), and demand price elastic, then a devaluation should increase incomes of some of the poor income classes of

---

[1]   Our previous simulations of trade liberalization published in IBRD, Morocco: Industrial Incentives and Export Promotion, 1984 (pp 63-74) using an heuristic framework showed that eliminating the SIT which would entail a reduction of 17.2% of import taxes, and devaluing by the same percentage would improve the balance of payments by $413 million, exports would increase by 12%, GDP by about 4$ and the budgetary deficit would deteriorate by DH 1,780 million. All these effects are very much in the range of the CGE estimations.

[2]   See UNICEF, 1984 "The Impact of World Recession on Children: A UNICEF Special Study", in the State of the World's Children 1984, Oxford U.P., 1984 and J. Behrman, "The Impact of Economic Adjustment Programs on Health and Nutrition in Developing Countries", 1986.

the society from the factor intensity side. If most of the staple food consumed by urban poor is imported, then the increase in import prices would certainly produce a reduction in their real income, unless food subsidies or other compensatory programs are stepped up. However, the income of farmers and landless rural laborers producing those staples would increase. The increase in prices in industrial import-substitution sectors might increase the incomes of specific factors and there is no presumption about its impact on the poor. There is also no clear indication on the impact of contractionary aggregate demand policies. Most important are changes in the structure of government receipts or expenditures.

196. It is presumed that most of the income redistribution occurring in a developing country is through government expenditures. Let us discuss each one in some detail. First, reducing food subsidies would have a substantial impact on real income of the urban poor[1]. However, it has been shown that food subsidies are very inefficient means of transferring income to the poor and targeting can have a large pay-off. The targeting can be made through food stamps, school lunches, baby feeding, and direct food aid. If those programs are already the most important means of transferring income to the poor, then curtailing their budget allowance would have a negative effect on the poor. The same would apply to basic health programs. To the extent that the main asset of the poor members of society is their human capital, moreover, cuts in health, nutrition and educational programs from which they benefit are likely to have negative longer-run effects on their future command over real resources.

197. Putting ceilings in overall government employment would not have a major impact on the poor since the groups most affected would be the educated youth. Cuts in government investment might have very different outcomes on the poor and it depends on the type of projects being curtailed. Finally, cuts in profit tax loopholes or in subsidies to irrigated water would decrease mostly the income of the upper income class.

198. To the extent that the Moroccan CGE has an household decomposition by socio-economic classes, it is possible to have some idea about the impact on agricultural and urban workers households. For a more detailed analysis, a greater disaggregation would be needed. A useful indicator is the evolution, in constant prices, of household expenditures. In the case of a 10% devaluation, agricultural households decrease their expenditures by 2.2%, while urban workers increase them by 0.7%. A cut of 10% in government consumption, in terms of public sector employment across-the-board, leads to a decrease of 6.9% in urban workers expenditures. A cut in government investment of 10% leads also to a reduction of 0.8% in urban workers expenditures. Both of these programs have a slight positive impact on

---

[1] See "Morocco: Compensatory Programs for Reducing Food Subsidies", 1986, where the elimination of DH 3 billion in food subsidies would cause a decrease of up to 20% in the real income of the urban poor.

agricultural households. A typical stabilization package relying more on devaluation and less in government investment or employment cuts would have a less depressive effect on the urban poor. An increase in overall domestic commodity taxation would have almost the same impact across all urban households, but will affect much less agricultural households.

199.   The effects of trade liberalization are interesting. Lifting quotas and other quantitative restrictions presumably would have a major impact on the income of the group to which the quota premia and rent-seeking activities accrue. Overall, the trade liberalization package induces a decrease of 1.7% in the expenditure of the urban poor without effects on the agricultural households. However, the introduction of a compensatory devaluation increases the welfare of the urban poor by 0.6% and decreases the agricultural household expenditures by 1%. The agricultural reform proposed above does not seem to have any noticeable impact on the status of the poor classes, except some increase in income to cereal producers.

7.3 Conclusions and Limitations of Results of the Models

200.   The role of this study was to clarify and quantify the role of stabilization and "supply side" policies in the adjustment process. The simulations presented above illustrate that a computable general equilibrium model is useful in tracing the effects of the most common stabilization and adjustment packages. To the extent that the model incorporates the institutional characteristics and uses a detailed and relatively updated data base, it can be used to guide the judgement of policy makers. On the theoretical side, the most interesting innovations of the model were the introduction of a "mark-up price rule" in protected sectors of the economy, and the stress in structural changes in the model when certain structural policies are pursued.

201.   Some of the most interesting results are: i) the important role played by devaluation in the stabilization and adjustment programs, which implies the adoption of a relatively flexible policy vis-a-vis the exchange rate; ii) supply side policies, also known as structural adjustment, can play a major role in easing the costs of adjustment and laying the foundations for a long-term sustained growth; iii) among adjustment policies, the ones which would have a major medium-term impact on the efficiency of the real economy seem to be: trade liberalization, fiscal reform, public expenditure restructuring and agricultural reform; iv) stabilization policies need to be closely coordinated with structural policies in order to reach the proposed targets in terms of internal and external re-equilibrium; and v) the social costs of adjustment cannot be ignored and may be very different across different policy designs. For example, the impact of devaluation is fundamentally different from the immpact of an across-the-board cut in government employment. But the most important costs can occur due to sectoral measures such as restructuring of public expenditures (e.g. cut in social welfare programs).

202. The framework used has, naturally, several limitations. First, the model only captures the real side of the economy: money and financial assets and flows that are important in stabilization policies are completely left out. The reason was the lack of data and theoretical difficulties in the integration of money in general equilibrium analysis. Second, the problem of lags and expectation formation is not dealt with formally. The user of the model would have to judge in each policy simulation if the change in economic environment would warrant changes in some parameters or variables and introduce them exogenously. The manipulation of supply and demand elasticities is the most important instrument to adapt to each horizon and introduce the results of the lags.

ANNEX I

THE PHOSPHATE SECTOR AND MARKET

1.   Although exports of phosphates are treated as exogenous in the CGE model, it is important to generate prices and quantities from a world phosphate market to plug into the model. The phosphate sector still dominates the Moroccan economy. Morocco is the world's leading exporter of phosphate rock and is endowed with the world's largest reserves of phoshpates. In the 1980s, Morocco has embarked in a strategy of diversifying and increasing domestic value added of its phosphate exports by installing a large capacity for producing phosphoric acid and fertilizers. Generating only about 7% of total value added, phosphates and its derivatives represent 42.2% of exports of goods (22% of phosphate rock, 14% of phosphoric acid and 6.2% of fertilizers) and contribute 21% to total government revenues (1985 data).

2.   At the beginning of the 1970s Morocco's share in world exports of phosphate rock awas around 30%. At the end of the 1970s it had increased to 34%, and this share has been maintained through the 1980s. After sustained growth in the 1960-78 period (5.5% p.a.) world trade volumes of phosphate rock decreased to an annual rate of 2.4% in 1978-83. In constant terms, prices of phosphate rock decreased almost steadily from 1955 to 1973. In the "phosphate price boom" of 1974-76 prices increased threefold, only to return afterwards to the late 1960s level. There was also a milder cycle (see graph) in the 1979-82 period.

3.   Phosphate rock is one of the main inputs in the production of phosphoric acid (the other is sulphur). One of the most important uses of phosphoric acid is the production of fertilizers. Since fertilizers are widely used in the production of wheat in industrialized countries, it would be expected that the price of phosphate rock and wheat would be highly correlated. An inspection of graphs I and II confirms the hypothesis.

4.   The purpose of this section is to build a simple world supply-demand model for phosphate rock with endogenous price expectations (quasi-rational). We start from a profit and cost function for wheat:

$$\Pi_W = \Pi(P_W; W_A, P_{PH}, P_W, P_N, P_K, P_E)$$

$$C_W = C(W_A, P_{PH}, P_N, P_K, P_E; Y_W)$$

where the profit function, Π, is a function of wheat prices, P_W, agricultural wage rates, W_A, prices of the different fertilizers: phosphoric, P_{PH}, nitrogeneous, P_N, and calcium, P_K, and the price of energy, P_E. The cost function is also function of the prices of inputs and level of production of wheat, Y_W.

5. From the cost function for wheat we can derive the demand function for phosphoric fertilizers, and from this demand function we obtain a derived demand function for phosphate rock, g_{PH}:

$$g_{PH} = d\,(P_{PH}^e,\ P_N,\ P_K,\ W_A,\ P_E;\ Y_W)$$

Deriving from the profit function for wheat the supply function for wheat and substituting, we obtain:

$$g_{PH}^D = d\,(P_{PH}^e,\ P_N,\ P_K,\ W,\ P_E,\ P_{IV},\ Y_{OECD})$$

where Y_{OECD} is the GDP of OECD countries.

6. Now a reasonable specification of the supply function of phosphate rock would depend on its expected price and the marginal costs of extraction:

$$g_{PH}^S = s\,(P_{PH}^e,\ p,\ P_E,\ W_M,\ d)$$

where r is the rate of interest, P_E price of energy, W_M the wage rate in the mining sector and d a rate of depletion.

7. Finally, price expectations for phosphate rock would depend, in a quasi-rational model of contemporaneous and lagged prices of wheat, on the prices of competing fertilizers:

$$P_{PH}^e = P\,(P_V,\ P_{W-1},\ P_{W-2},\ P_N,\ P_K)$$

8. In the implementation of the model we took for wage rates and the rate of depletion data for the USA. The model was estimated by 2SLS using yearly data from 1963 to 1980. Three functional forms (linear, double-log, and yearly percentage changes) were used to estimate the price, demand, and supply equations.

9. The results are presented in Table I. The derived price and income elasticities are presented in Table II. The price of phosphate is strongly, and positively linked to the price of wheat (current and lagged). The price of wheat lagged two periods has no effect and was dropped from the equation. The price of nitrogenous fertilizer has a positive effect on the price of phosphate.

10. The demand for phosphates is strongly related to all the explanatory variables.[1/] However, it should be noted that even if all the coefficients are statistically significant, their magnitudes are low. Moreover, the magnitude of the incercept term is very high. This could suggest that some important variables are omitted in the specification of the demand equation. The positive relationship between the price of nitrogenous fertilizer and the demand for phosphate supports the hypothesis that phosphate and nitrogen are substitutes. The same thing can be said about phosphate and labor. The price of wheat was dropped from the demand equation because it creates severe collinearity problems.

1/ The price of energy was dropped from the equation because its effect is insignificant.

GRAPH I

WHEAT

(YEARLY AVERAGE)

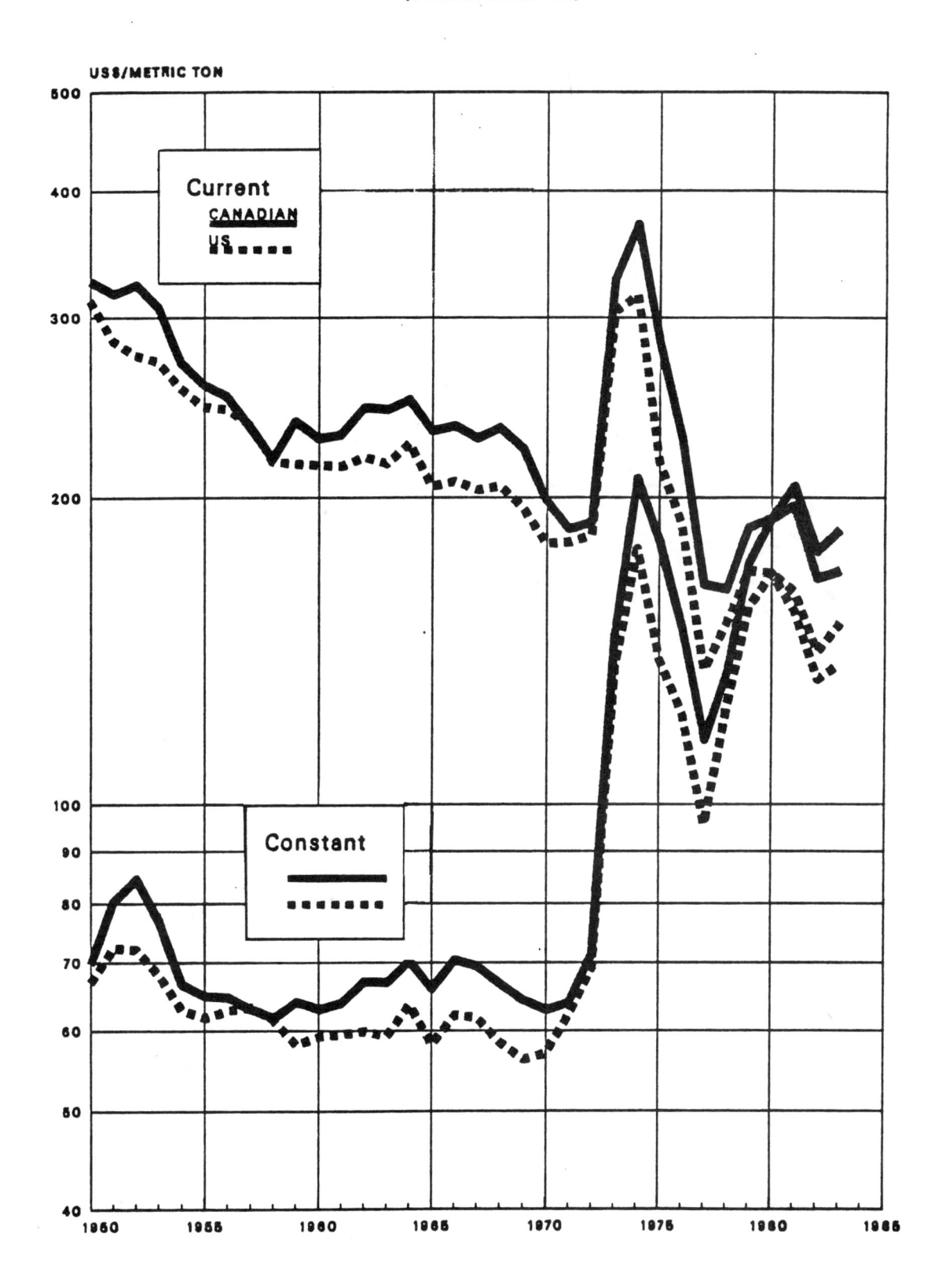

GRAPH II

PHOSPHATE ROCK

(YEARLY AVERAGE)

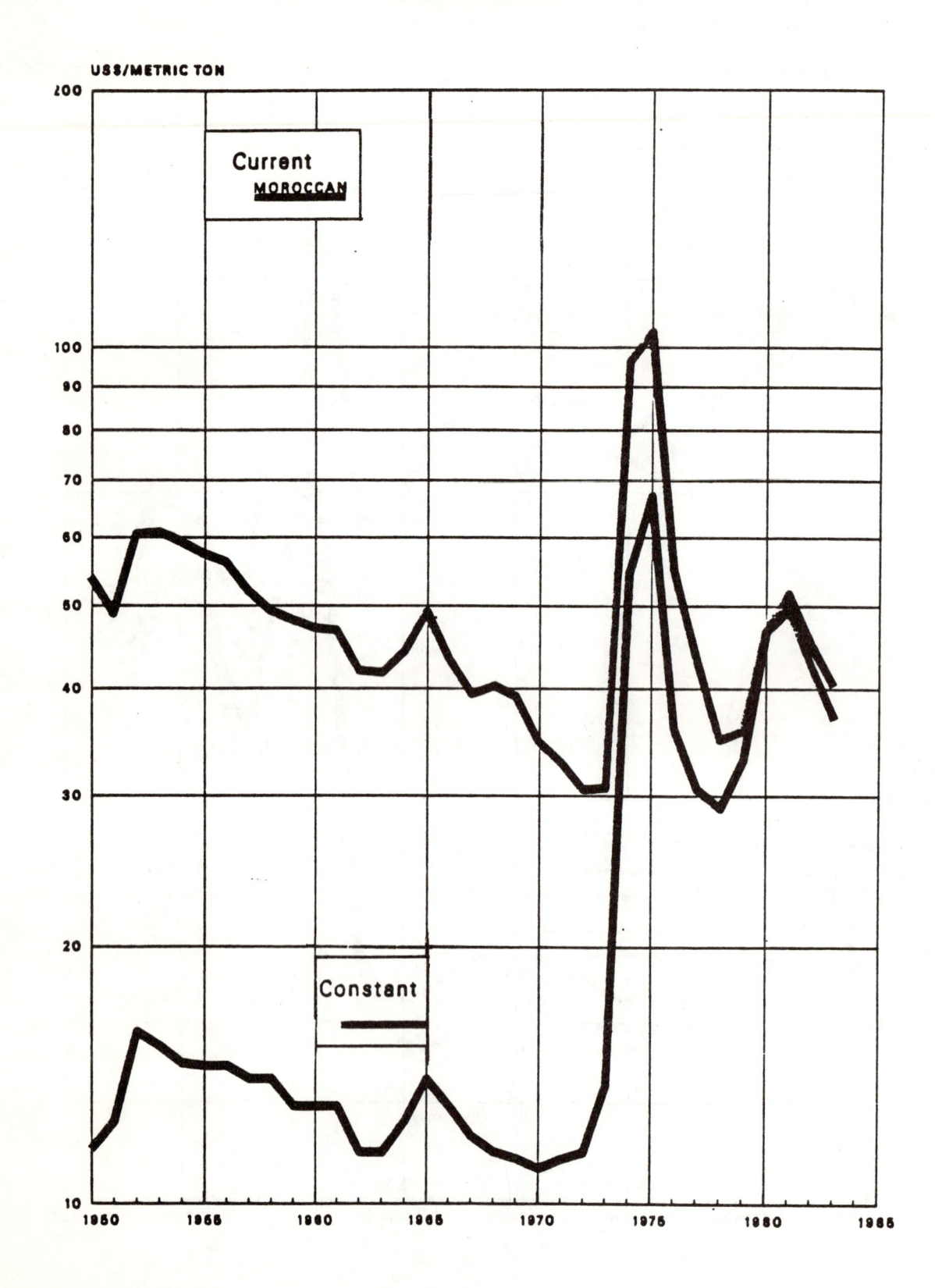

11. It was not possible to accurately identify the supply equation. As can be seen from Table I, the price of phosphate has a negative effect on the supply of phosphates, a fact that contradicts economic theory. The derived income and price elasticities for the supply function, should, therefore, be interpreted with care.

12. The negative price effect on the supply equation can be due to the various shocks the phosphate sector experienced during the 1970s. A few downward shifts might have occurred in the supply curve during that period. What we are identifying is the series of structural changes that occurred in the 1970s rather than the supply curve.

Table I: ESTIMATES OF THE WORLD SUPPLY DEMAND MODEL FOR PHOSPHATE ROCK
(t-ratios are in parentheses)

	Price lin.form	Price log.form	Demand lin.form	Demand log.form	Supply lin.form	Supply log.form
Intercept	−5.716 (.050)	.031 (.315)	8.597 (.299)	.502 (2.807)	143.406 (4.418)e	11.090
Price of Phosphate	−	− (3.150)	−.124 (3.370)	−.200 (3.133)	−.106 (3.457)	−.186
Price of Wheat	−.649 (3.414)	−6.757 (2.725)	−	−	−	−
Price of Wheat lagged	1.249	1.596 (5.786)	(5.841)	−	−	−
Price of Nitrogen	.164	.006 (1.553)	.063 (.162)	.037 (2.433)	− (1.628)	−
Wage Rate Ag. Sector	−	−	.340 (1.130)	.037 (1.633)	−	−
Wage Rate Mining Sector	−	−	−	−	−.557 (1.059)	−1.411 (2.551)
Wheat Production (Proxy for income)	−	−	.534 (3.052)	.405 (2.015)	−	−
Interest Rate (US)	−	−	−	−	1.237 (1.565)	−1.992 (1.992)
Depletion Rate of Phosphate Reserves	−	−	−	−	.040 (1.359)	.142 (4.368)
R^2	.85	.85	.72	.72	.81	.85
DW	1.59	1.986	1.781	1.772	1.808	1.819
Root Mean Square Error	33.15	.176	7.05	.092	4.136	.04

Table II: PRICE AND INCOME ELASTICITIES[a] FOR THE SUPPLY
AND DEMAND OF PHOSPHATE ROCK
(From the linear form)

	Demand	Supply
Price Phosphate	−.43	−
Price Nitrogen	.18	−
Wage Rate/Agriculture	−	.43
Wage Rate/Mining	−	−.851
Interest Rate (US)	−	−.004
Depletion Rate	−	.08
Wheat Production (Income proxy)	.66	−

a/ Computed at sample means.

ANNEX II

A. MATHEMATICAL STRUCTURE OF THE MODEL

CORE MODEL

Outline of model structure

Dimensions

34 (12)	commodities and activities
8 (3)	nontraded goods sectors
2	types of value added: formal and informal sector
5	labor categories
19	types of capital
4	types of household

Production

CES-CD value added functions for each industry.

Fixed input-output coefficient intermediate production.

Fixed coefficient joint production.

Demand

Linear expenditure system for household consumption.

Investment and government consumption exogenous.

Export demand function (constant elasticity) and exogenous for phosphates or exports subject to quotas.

Taxes

Indirect domestic taxes -- PTS, TIC and other minor taxes.

Import taxes -- custom duties, TSI, and other minor taxes.

Direct taxes -- TPS (labor tax), PSN, complementary tax.

Profit taxes -- IBP and PSN on enterprises.

Social security -- payments to social security by employers and employees.

Subsidies

Consumer subsidies.

Equilibrium

Set of equilibrium prices such that

(i) Demands equal supplies for all goods and factors.

(ii) All rows and columns of the SAM are balanced, which means implicitly that:

(a) zero non-normal profits in each industry (after taxes);

(b) external balance (after capital inflow) holds;

(c) government sector revenues equal payments (after deficit financing).

2. Production

(i) Value added functions (CES)

$$Y_j = \left[\delta_j K_j^{-\rho_j} + (1-\delta_j) L_j^{-\rho_j} \right]^{-1/\rho_j}$$

j = AGREXP; AGRP-S; AGRP-O; INDEXP;

(ii) Labor aggregation (two-level CES):

(a) Aggregation of nonskilled (I) and semiskilled (II) workers.

$$L_{AJ} = \left[\delta_j^A L_{Ij}^{-\rho_j} + (1-\delta_j^I) L_{IIj}^{-\rho_j} \right]^{-1/\rho_j}$$

(b) Aggregation of workers (A) and technostructure (B).

$$L_j = \left[\delta_j^A L_{A_j}^{-\rho_j} + (1-\delta_j^A) L_{B_j}^{-\rho_j}\right]^{-1/\rho_j}$$

j = PHOSPH; PETROL; INDEXP; INDSF; INDS-0; INDIMP; PROTEC

(iii) Intermediate production requirements (fixed coefficients)

$$X_{ij} = a_{ij} X_j$$

(iv) Joint production of commodities (fixed coefficients)

$$J_{ij} = \gamma_{ij} X_j \;;$$

$$\sum_i \gamma_{ij} = -1, \; 0$$

3. <u>Consumer demands and incomes</u>

(i) Linear expenditure system

Consumption of the ith commodity by households of type k is given by:

$$C_{ik} = \left[\gamma_{ik} + \beta_{ik}(1-s_k) YD_k\right]/q_i$$

for all k, where

$$Y_{ik} = q_i \hat{Y}_{ik} - \beta_{ik} \sum_i q_i \hat{Y}_{ik} .$$

(ii) Disposable income

Disposable income of household k is defined as the sum of payments to labor (w_j), distributed profits (π_j), transfers from the treasury (TG), payments of dividends (D_j), social security transfers (TS) and transfers from the rest of the world (TX). The items to deduct are social security payments by employees (PS) and direct taxes (TD). Other items like inter-household transfers and transfers to the rest of the world can also be included:

$$YD_k = \sum_j (W_{jk} + \pi_{jk} + D_{jk}) + TG_k + TS_k + TX_k - \sum_j PS_{kj} - TD_k .$$

4. Industry and import factor demand

(i) Industry production levels function of prices which meet commodity demands (commodity balances).

$$X(P) = [I-A]^{-1} F(P) .$$

(ii) Import demand.

Import demand is derived from a CES production function between domestic production and imported goods (Armingtonian assumption):

$$X_j = \left[\delta_j X_j^{-\rho} + (1-\delta_j) M_j^{-\rho} \right]^{-1/\rho_j}$$

from which we can derive a demand function for imports

$$M_j = (1-\delta_j)^\sigma (P_M/P)^{-\sigma} X_j$$

(iii) Derived demand for factors.

From a CES production function, the following derived demand for labor and capital are derived:

$$L_j(\rho) = \delta_j^\sigma \left(\frac{w_j(1+t_j^L)}{r_j(1+t_j^K)} \right)^{-\sigma} X_j$$

$$K_j(\rho) = (1-\delta_j)^\sigma \left(\frac{r_j(1+t_j^K)}{w_j(1+t_j^L)} \right)^{-\sigma} X_j$$

5. <u>Export demand functions</u>

Export demand functions of constant elasticity are specified for industry and agriculture sectors that are export oriented.

$$E_j = E_j^o \left(\frac{P_j}{\pi_j} \right)^{-\eta}$$

P_j are export prices and π_j world prices for product j. For a small country, this formulation can be criticized. However, it has been extensively used by Dervis, de Melo, and Robinson[1]/, with the justification that in a world with product differentiation, the demand for an export product is not perfectly elastic.

6. Producer prices, consumer prices, and taxes

With constant returns to scale and no joint production, the producer price of good i is equal to its unit cost of production.

$$(1) \quad P_i = \sum_{j=1}^{n} a_{ji}q_{ji} + \sum_{f=1}^{m} (1+\sigma_f)v_{fi} + \xi_i \qquad V_i p$$

In the case of fully traded goods, trade arbitrage gives

$$(2) \quad P_i = (1+\tau_i)e\pi_i; \qquad\qquad i \in t. \ P$$

but to eliminate arbitrage between different users of the same good requires an effective regulation.

In the short run, it seems reasonable to assume that all input-output ratios are fixed. Hence, given the user costs of goods to the sectors producing fully traded goods and the taxes ξ, total factor costs in those sectors fall into line with the exogenously determined producer price, as given by (2). In the case of nontraded goods, however, we need some other rule governing the relation between producer prices and factor costs. A simple and appealing assumption is that the

---

[1]/ See Dervis, de Melo and Robinson, *General Equilibrium Models for Planning*, 1982, Johns Hopkins University Press, Chapter VII.

'nominal' wage is constant and profits are a constant mark-up over prime cost plus sector-specific taxes. Hence,

$$(3) \quad \lambda_i = \phi_i P_i \qquad\qquad i \in N$$

where ϕ_i is related to the mark-up constant, μ_i, by $\mu_i = \phi_i/(1-\phi_i)$ and

$$(4) \quad \lambda_i = \sum_{f=1}^{m'} (1+\sigma_f)\sigma_f,$$

where the factors are ordered such that the first m' of them refer to 'capital' of one kind or another.

Define the sector-specific tax rates on intermediate goods as

$$(5) \quad t_{ij} = \frac{q_{ij} - P_i}{P_i}.$$

Equation (1) may be rewritten as

$$(6) \quad P_i = \sum_{j=1}^{n} a_{ji}(1+t_{ji})P_j + \sum_{f=m'+1}^{m} w_f \ell_{fi} + \lambda_i - \xi_i$$

for all i. Also, in view of (2) and (3),

$$(7) \quad P_i = \sum_{j \in T} a_{ji}(1-t_{ji})(1+t_j)e\pi_j + \sum_{j \in N} a_{ji}(1+t_{ji})P_j + \phi_i P_i$$

$$\qquad\qquad + \sum_{f=m'+1}^{m} (1+\sigma_f)w_f \ell_{fi} + \xi_i \qquad i \in N$$

Inspection of (7) reveals that if $\{a_{ij}, \ell_{fi}, w_f, t_{ji}, \tau_j, \pi_j, \phi_i, \xi_i\}$ are known, then the prices of nontraded goods can be derived at once by matrix inversion, the prices of fully traded goods being given by (2).

Having found producer prices, industrial user prices $\{q_{ij}\}$ and consumer prices $\{p_i\}$ follow at once from the set of commodity tax rates, which are parametrically given.

So much for the determination of goods prices. The next step is to deal with the distribution of value added among the various factors of production. Let the share of each type of capital payments to capital be constant. Define

$$(8) \qquad \alpha_{fj} = (1+\sigma_f)vf/\lambda_j, \qquad f = 1, \ldots, m'$$

where, by definition, $\sum_f \alpha_{fj} = 1$ and α_{fj} is constant (all f,j). Denote the gross output, in "quantity" units, of sector j by O_j. Then the total cost of capital of type f is simply

$$(9) \qquad W_f = \sum_j \alpha_{fj} \lambda_j O_j \qquad f = 1, \ldots, m'.$$

where λ_j is given by

$$(10) \qquad \lambda_j = \begin{cases} P_j - \sum_i a_{ij}(1+t_{ij})P_i - \sum_{f=m'+1}^{m'} (1+\sigma_f)w_f \ell_{fs} - \xi_j, & j \in T \\ \phi_j P_j, & j \in N \end{cases}$$

In the case of labor,

(11) $\quad w_f = \sum_j (1+\sigma_f) w_f \ell_{fj} 0_j \quad\quad\quad f = m' + 1, \ldots, m.$

A fraction $1/(1-\sigma_f)$ is paid to the owners of f, with the remainder going to the treasury as employment/social security taxes.

The long run

We now permit some substitution, with factor ratios being chosen by profit maximizing agents. [1] In order to keep matters tractable, we shall assume that production possibilities in each industry can be represented by a two-level production function in capital, labor and intermediates, in which there is no substitutability within the set of intermediate goods, but intermediates as a group are substitutable for labor and capital in Cobb-Douglas form.

Let X_i denote the index volume of all intermediate goods used in industry i and let q_i^o denote its price. Then

(12) $\quad q_i^o = \dfrac{\sum_j a_{ji} q_{ji}}{\sum_j a_{ji}},$

and

---

[1] In the case of public enterprises, other behavioral assumptions are more attractive, but that matter is left for discussion.

(13) $$Q_i = A_i K_i^{\sigma_{i1}} L_i^{\sigma_{i2}} X_i^{1-\sigma_{i1}-\sigma_{i2}}$$

where A_i is a shift parameter and only one sort each of capital and labor are used for simplicity of exposition. The first order conditions for profit maximization are

(14) $$\alpha_{1i} P_i Q_i = r_i K_i,$$

(15) $$\alpha_{2i} P_i Q_i = w_i L_i,$$

(16) $$\alpha_{3i} P_i Q_i = q_i^o X_i,$$

where $\alpha_{3i} = 1 - \alpha_{1t} - \alpha_{2i}$. Note that wage and profit rates may vary across industries.

In the case of fully traded goods, we know that P_i is given by

(2) $$P_i = (1 + \tau_i) e \pi_i, \qquad i \varepsilon T$$

The material balances may be written in the form

(17) $$Q = AQ - C + E + J + G,$$

where

$A = A(p, r, w, q^o)$ and $C = C(Y, q)$. Income (value added) is given by

(18) $Y = r'K + w'L.$

Without going into the details of taxes, subsidies and transfers, it is clear that there are two cases to be dealt with. First, if government consumption, G, and total investment, J, are set equal in value to domestic savings (net of foreign debt-service payments), the external account will be in balance and it is easily verified that one of the foregoing equations can be deduced from the rest. That is, of course, a particular statement of Walrus' Law. Second, if any elements of G and/or J are set exogenously in such a way as to require that foreign savings be endogenous, the degree of freedom in question is restored. We now examine these cases in greater detail.

In the first case, G and J are functions of incomes and prices, though the precise specification need not detain us here. For $i \in N$, E_i is exogenous (usually zero); for $i \in \mathcal{E}$, however, E_i is endogenous, and the question of how its scale and that of the associated output Q_i are to be determined must be addressed. As the traverse from the short run to the long run will be handled in an <u>ad hoc</u> manner, it seems attractive to limit the scale of the entire system by setting an overall constraint on the capital stock, viz.,

$$(19) \quad \sum_i K_i = \bar{K}$$

A little reflection reveals, however, that this is not enough. Given (p, r, w, q^o), output is indeterminate in a CRS economy. Suppose $\underline{K}^*$ satisfying (19) is a solution and consider a small perturbation in the allocations among $i \epsilon T$. It seems likely that (19) will continue to hold if the perturbation is made appropriately, while w, r, p, etc. stay constant. Moreover, since savings determine investment, the foreign account will remain in balance. Hence, the chances are that equilibrium is not locally unique in the case where w and r are exogenous, which is the case of interest to us. The obvious alternative is to set the capital stocks in the sectors producing tradable goods exogenously, while allowing those in the sectors producing nontradables to come out in the wash, that is,

$$(20) \quad K_i = \bar{K}_i \qquad i \epsilon T,$$

which would replace (19).

The second case would be identical, except that foreign savings would be endogenous in the face of exogenous investment and/or government consumption.

To sum up, given w, r, π, taxes, tariffs, E_N, K_T, and the exchange rate, we are to determine the following endogenous variables:

$$P, q^o, Q, K_N, L, X, E_T \text{ and } Y,$$

with J and G **exogenous** or endogenous as desired.

NOTATION

P_i producer price of good i

π_i world price of good i

q_{ij} cost of a unit of good i to producers in industry j

q_j^o cost of an index unit of intermediate goods used in industry j

q_i price of good i to households

ξ_j tax on industry j when it is operating at unit intensity (ex. commodity taxes)

v_{fj} payment to factor f by industry j when j is working at unity intensity

σ_f tax levied on employers of factor f (per unit payment to factor f)

π_i world price of good i

τ_i tariff rate on good i

B. SECTOR SPECIFICATION

TRADABLES

Type I: Price adjustment plus limited isolation from world markets

Supply side:

(1) Supply of goods to activities:

$$\sum_i X^D_{ji} = Z^D_i$$

(2) Domestic production combined with imports:

$$X_{ji} = \left[\delta_i (X^D_{ji})^{-\rho} + (1-\delta_i) M_i^{-\rho}\right]^{\frac{1}{1-\rho}}$$

(3) Production function among variable factors:

$$V_i = \min\left[\frac{L_i}{\alpha_i} \;;\; \frac{X_{ji}}{a_{ji}}\right]$$

(4) Production function among fixed and variable factors:

$$Z^D_i = \left[\delta_i \bar{K}_i^{-\rho} + (1-\delta_i) V_i^{-\rho}\right]^{\frac{1}{1-\rho}}$$

(fixed capital)

Demand side:

(5) Household consumption:

$$C_i = f(P_i/P, Y)$$

(6) Exports of goods and services:

$$E_i = E_{io}(P_i/\pi_i)^{-\eta} \quad \text{or} \quad E_i = \bar{E}_i .$$

Price model:

(7) Determination of domestic price:

$$P_i = C_i(P_i) + E_i(P_i) - M_i(P_i) + \bar{J}_i + \bar{G}_i = 0$$

(8) Determination of profit rate:

$$\lambda_i = P_i - \ell_i \bar{w}_i (1+G_f) - \sum_j a_{ij} P_j (1+\zeta_j) - \sum_j a^*_{ij} \pi_j (1+\zeta_j + \tau_j)$$

Type II: Production exogenous; domestic price determined by world price.

Supply side:

(1) Supply of goods to activities:

$$\sum_i X^D_{ji} = \bar{Z}^D_i$$

(2) Domestic production combined with imports ($\rho = \infty$).

$$X_{ji} = X^D_{ji} + M_i$$

(3) Production function among variable factors:

$$V_i = \min \left[\frac{L_i}{\alpha_i}, \frac{X_{ji}}{a_{ji}} \right]$$

(4) Residual profits:

$$\Pi_i = Z^D_i - V_i$$

Demand side (exports, government consumption, exogenous):

(5) Household consumption:

$$C_i = f(P_i/p, Y)$$

Price model:

(6) Determination of profit rate:

$$\lambda_i = \Pi_i - \ell_i \bar{w}_i (1+G_i) - \sum_j a_{ij} P_j (1+t^{1D}_j) - \sum_j a^*_{ij} \Pi_j (1+t^{1D}+\tau_j)$$

Type IIA: Production exogenous and domestic price adjustment

Supply side:

(1) Supply of goods to activities:

$$\sum_i X^D_{ji} = \bar{Z}^D_i$$

(2) Domestic production combined with imports:

$$X_{ji} = \left[\delta_i(X^D_{ji})^{-\rho} + (1-\delta_i)M_i^{-\rho}\right]^{\frac{1}{1-\rho}}$$

(3) Production function among variable factors:

$$V_i = \min\left[\frac{L_i}{\alpha_i}, \frac{X_{ji}}{a_{ji}}\right]$$

(4) Residual profits:

$$\Pi_i = Z^D_i - V_i$$

Demand side: (exports, government consumption exogenous)

(5) Household consumption:

$$C_i = f(P_i/P, Y)$$

Price model:

(6) Determination of domestic price:

$$P_i = C_i(P_i) + E_i(P_i) - M_i(P_i) + \bar{J}_i + \bar{G}_i = 0$$

(7) Determination of profit rate:

$$\pi_i = P_i - \ell_i \bar{w}_i(1+G_i) - \sum_j a_{ij} P_j(1+\varepsilon_j) - \sum_j a^*_{ij} \pi_j(1+\varepsilon_j+\tau_j)$$

SECTOR SPECIFICATION

<u>Type III</u>: Domestic price administered; demand determines quantity

Supply side:

(1) Supply of goods to activities:

$$\sum_i X^D_{ji} = Z^D_i$$

(2) Domestic production combined with imports:

$$X_{ji} = X^D_{ji} + \bar{M}_i$$

(3) Production function among variable factors:

$$V_i = \min \left[\frac{L_i}{\alpha_i} \; ; \; \frac{X_{ji}}{\alpha_{ji}} \right]$$

(4) Production function among fixed and variable factors:

$$Z^D_i = \left[\delta_i K_i^{-\rho} + (1-\delta_i) V_i^{-\rho} \right]^{\frac{1}{1-\rho}} \qquad \rho = \infty$$

Demand side:

(5) Household consumption:

$$C_i = f(P_i/P, Y)$$

(6) Exports of goods and services:

$$E_i = \bar{E}_i$$

Price model:

(7) Domestic price controlled:

$$P_i = \bar{P}_i$$

Type IIIA: Domestic price determined by world price plus tariff; external trade adjusts market

Supply side:

(1) Supply of goods to activities:

$$\sum_i X^D_{ji} = Z^D_i$$

(2) Domestic production combined with imports:

$$X_{ji} = X^D_{ji} + M_i$$

(3) Production function among variable factors:

$$V_i = \min \left[\frac{L_i}{\alpha_i} ; \frac{X_{ji}}{a_{ji}} \right]$$

(4) Production function among fixed and variable factors:

$$Z^D_i \left[\delta_i K_i^{-\rho} + (1-\delta_i) V_i^{-\rho} \right]^{\frac{1}{1-\rho}}$$

Demand side:

(5) Household consumption:

$$C_i = f(P_i, Y)$$

(6) Exports of goods and services:

$$E_i = \bar{E}_i$$

Price model:

(7) Determination of domestic price:

$$P_i = \ell_i \bar{w}_i (1+\sigma_i) + \sum_j a_{ij} P_j (1+t^{1D}_j) + \sum_j a_{ij} \Pi_j (1+t^{1D} + \tau_j)$$

Type IV: Price and quantity are fixed

Supply side:

(1) Supply of good to activities:

$$\sum_i X^D_{ji} = \bar{Z}^D_i$$

(2) Production function among variable factors:

$$V_i = \min \left[\frac{L_i}{\alpha_i} ; \frac{X_{ji}}{a_{ji}} \right]$$

Demand side:

(3) Inter-industrial demand:

$$Z^D_i \sum_j a_{ij} X_j$$

Price model:

(4) Determination of domestic prices:

$$P_i = \bar{P}_i$$

Type V: Domestic price determined by supply and demand; world price plus tariff

Supply side:

(1) Supply of goods to activities:

$$\sum_i X^D_{ji} = Z^D_i$$

(2) Domestic production combined with imports:

$$X_{ji} = \left[\delta_i (X^D_{ji})^{-\rho} + (1-\delta_i)\bar{M}_i^{-\rho}\right]^{\frac{1}{1-\rho}}$$

(3) Production function among variable factors:

$$V_i = \min\left[\frac{L_i}{\alpha_i} \; ; \; \frac{X_{ij}}{a_{ji}}\right]$$

(4) Production function among fixed and variable factors:

$$Z^D_i = \left[\delta_i K_i^{-\rho} + (1-\delta_i)V_i^{-\rho}\right]^{\frac{1}{1-\rho}}$$

Demand side:

(5) Household consumption:

$$C_i = f(P_i/P, Y)$$

(6) Exports of goods and services:

$$E_i = E_{io}(P_i/\Pi_i)^{-\eta}$$

Price model:

(7) Determination of domestic price:

$$P_i = C_i(P_i) + E_i(P_i) - \bar{M}_i + \bar{J}_i + \bar{G}_i = 0$$

(8) Determination of profit rate:

$$\pi_i = P_i - \ell_i \bar{w}_i(1+\sigma_i) - \sum_j a_{ij} P_j(1+t^{1D}) - \sum_j a_{ij} \pi_j P_j(1+t^{1D} + \tau_i)$$

<u>Type VA</u>: Domestic price determined by world price plus tariff; external trade adjusts market

Supply side:

(1) Supply of goods to activities:

$$\sum_i X^D_{ji} = Z^D_i$$

(2) Domestic production combined with imports:

$$X_{ji} = X^D_{ji} + \bar{M}_i$$

(3) Production function among variable factors:

$$V_i = \min \left[\frac{L_i}{\alpha_i} ; \frac{X_{ji}}{a_{ji}} \right]$$

(4) Production function among fixed and variable factors:

$$Z^D_i = \left[\delta_i \bar{K}_i^{-\rho} + (1-\delta_i) V_i^{-\rho} \right]^{\frac{1}{1-\rho}}$$

Demand side:

(5) Household consumption:

$$C_i = f(P_i/P, Y)$$

(6) Exports of goods and services:

$$E_i = \bar{E}_i$$

Price model:

(7) Determination of domestic price:

$$P_i = P_i(1+\tau_j)$$

Type VI: Protected sectors

Supply side:

(1) Supply of goods to activities:

$$\sum_i X^D_{ji} = Z^D_i$$

(2) Production function among variable factors:

$$V_i = \min \left[\frac{L_i}{\alpha_i} \; ; \; \frac{X_{ji}}{a_{ji}} \right]$$

Demand side:

(3) Household consumption:

$$C_i = f(P_i/P, Y)$$

Price model:

(4) Determination of domestic price (mark-up):

$$P_i = \left[\ell_i \bar{w}_i (1+\sigma_i) + \sum_j a_{ij} P_j (1+t_j^{1D}) + \sum_j a^*_{ij} \pi_j (1+t^{1D}+t_j) \right](1+\lambda)$$

Type VII: Petroleum

Supply side:

(1) Supply of goods to activities:

$$\sum_i X_{ji}^D = \bar{Z}_i^D$$

(2) Production function among variable factors (limited substitutability):

$$V_i = \min \left[\frac{L_i}{\alpha_i}, \frac{X_{ji}^*}{a_{ji}} \right]$$

(3) Complementarity between intermediate commodities and imports:

$$X_{ji}^* = \min \left[\frac{X_{ji}}{a_{ji}}, \frac{M_i}{m_i} \right]$$

(4) Residual profits:

$$\Pi_i = Z_i^O - V_i$$

Demand side:

(5) Household consumption:

$$C_i = f(P_i/P, Y)$$

(6) Exports, investment: exogenous:

Price model:

(7) Determination of domestic price:

$$P_i = \pi_i(1+\tau_i)$$

LIST OF VARIABLES

X^D_{ji} = Domestic production of sector j supplied to activity i;

Z^D_i = Activity level of sector i;

M_i = Imports of good i;

V_i = Aggregate of variable factors of production in sector i;

L_i = Labor input in sector i;

X_{ji} = Flow of intermediate goods from sector j to sector i;

K_i = Fixed capital (used in sector i);

C_i = Household consumption;

J_i = Investment;

G_i = Government consumption;

P_i = Price on sector i;

E_i = Exports of sector i;

π^*_i = World price on sector i;

λ_i = Profit rate in sector i;

G_i = Tax on labor in sector i;

t^{1D} = Indirect tax on sector i;

τ = Import tax on sector i;

w_i = Wage rate on sector i.

C. SUPPLY AND DEMAND ELASTICITIES IN THE MODEL

Deriving the supply function from a CES

Let us suppose we have the CES production function

$$y = \left[\sum_{i=1}^{N} \delta_i X_i^\rho \right]^{\mu/\rho}$$

where we have N inputs with prices $W_1, W_2, \ldots, W_N$, and output has the price p. The elasticity of substitution is $\sigma = \frac{1}{1-\rho}$, δ_i is a distribution parameter and μ measures returns to scale.

If $\mu = 1$, and inputs $1, \ldots, S$ are variable and $S+1, \ldots, N$ fixed, then the restricted profit function is:

$$\Pi = \left[p^{1-\sigma} - \sum_{i=1}^{S} \delta_i^\sigma (W_i)^{1-\sigma} \right]^{\frac{1}{1-\sigma}} \left[\sum_{s+1}^{N} \delta_i X_i^\rho \right]^{1/\rho}$$

if condition (ϱ): $p > \left[\sum_{1}^{S} \delta_i^\sigma w_i^{1-\sigma} \right]$ is verified.

This condition means that output prices cover variable unit costs. $\Pi = 0$, if condition (ϱ) is not verified for $0 < \sigma < 1$ and $\Pi = \infty$ if $\sigma > 1$.

The supply function is obtained by deriving the profit function in respect to the output price, p.

For $\mu < 1$ the supply function is

$$y = \mu^{\mu(1-\mu)^{-1}} \left[\sum_{1}^{S} \delta_i \left(\frac{W_i}{\delta} \right)^{\rho/(\rho-1)} \right]^{((1-\mu)^{-1}(\rho-1))/\rho}$$

If there are some inputs fixed then the normalized profit function may not have a closed form solution.[1]

Deriving trade elasticities

The Armingtonian Assumption specifies that imported goods and domestic goods are not perfect substitutes. The model uses a CES aggregation function of commodities produced abroad (imports, M_i) and commodities produced domestically, D_{i1}, for sector i:

$$Q_i = \bar{B}\left[\delta_i M_i^{-\rho_i} + (1-\delta_i)D_i^{-\rho_i}\right]^{-1/\rho_i}$$

with $\sigma_i = \frac{1}{1+\rho_i}$, , the sectoral "trade elasticity of substitution". Letting ρ_i denote the domestic price and Π_i the domestic currency price of imports, we can derive the following demand curve for imports:

$$M_i = \left(\frac{\delta_i}{1-\delta_i}\right)^{\sigma_i} \left(\frac{\rho_i}{\pi_i}\right)^{\sigma_i} D_i .$$

The import price elasticity is thus given by σ_i.

---

[1] See D. McFadden: Cost, Revenue and Profit Functions, in M. Furs and D. McFadden, ed., **Production Economics: A Dual Approach to Theory and Applications**, North-Holland, 1976.

DISTRIBUTORS OF WORLD BANK PUBLICATIONS

ARGENTINA
Carlos Hirsch, SRL
Galeria Guemes
Florida 165, 4th Floor-Ofc. 453/465
1333 Buenos Aires

AUSTRALIA, PAPUA NEW GUINEA, FIJI, SOLOMON ISLANDS, VANUATU, AND WESTERN SAMOA
Info-Line
Overseas Document Delivery
Box 506, GPO
Sydney, NSW 2001

AUSTRIA
Gerold and Co.
A-1011 Wien
Graben 31

BAHRAIN
MEMRB Information Services
P.O. Box 2750
Manama Town 317

BANGLADESH
Micro Industries Development Assistance Society (MIDAS)
G.P.O. Box 800
Dhaka

BELGIUM
Publications des Nations Unies
Av. du Roi 202
1060 Brussels

BRAZIL
Publicacoes Tecnicas Internacionais Ltda.
Rua Peixoto Gomide, 209
01409 Sao Paulo, SP

CANADA
Le Diffuseur
C.P. 85, 1501 Ampere Street
Boucherville, Quebec
J4B 5E6

COLOMBIA
Enlace Ltda.
Carrera 6 No. 51-21
Bogota D.E.

Apartado Aereo 4430
Cali, Valle

COSTA RICA
Libreria Trejos
Calle 11-13
Av. Fernandez Guell
San Jose

COTE D'IVOIRE
Entre d'Edition et de Diffusion Africaines (CEDA)
04 B.P. 541
Abidjan 04 Plateau

CYPRUS
MEMRB Information Services
P.O. Box 2098
Nicosia

DENMARK
SamfundsLitteratur
Rosenoerns Alle 11
DK-1970 Frederiksberg C.

DOMINICAN REPUBLIC
Editora Taller, C. por A.
Restauracion
Apdo. postal 2190
Santo Domingo

EGYPT, ARAB REPUBLIC OF
Al Ahram
Al Galaa Street
Cairo

FINLAND
Akateeminen Kirjakauppa
P.O. Box 128
SF-00101
Helsinki 10

FRANCE
World Bank Publications
66, avenue d'Iéna
75116 Paris

GERMANY, FEDERAL REPUBLIC OF
UNO-Verlag
Poppelsdorfer Alle 55
D-5300 Bonn 1

GREECE
KEME
24, Ippodamou Street
Athens-11635

GUATEMALA
Librerias Piedra Santa
Centro Cultural Piedra Santa
11 calle 6-50 zona 1
Guatemala City

HONG KONG, MACAU
Asia 2000 Ltd.
6 Fl., 146 Prince Edward Road, W,
Kowloon
Hong Kong

HUNGARY
Kultura
P.O. Box 139
1389 Budapest 62

INDIA
Allied Publishers Private Ltd.
751 Mount Road
Madras—600 002

15 J.N. Heredia Marg
Ballard Estate
Bombay—400 038

13/14 Asaf Ali Road
New Delhi—110 002

17 Chittaranjan Avenue
Calcutta—700 072

Jayadeva Hostel Building
5th Main Road Gandhinagar
Bangalore—560 009

3-5-1129 Kachiguda Cross Road
Hyderabad—500 027

Prarthana Flats, 2nd Floor
Near Thakore Baug, Navrangpura
Ahmedabad—380 009

Patiala House
16-A Ashok Marg
Lucknow—226 001

INDONESIA
Pt. Indira Limited
Jl. Sam Ratulangi 37
Jakarta Pusat
P.O. Box 181

IRELAND
TDC Publishers
12 North Frederick Street
Dublin 1

ISRAEL
The Jerusalem Post
The Jerusalem Post Building
P.O. Box 81
Romema Jerusalem 91000

ITALY
Licosa Commissionaria Sansoni SPA
Via Lamarmora 45
Casella Postale 552
50121 Florence

JAPAN
Eastern Book Service
37-3, Hongo 3-Chome, Bunkyo-ku 113
Tokyo

JORDAN
Jordan Center for Marketing Research
P.O. Box 3143
Jabal
Amman

KENYA
Africa Book Service (E.A.) Ltd.
P.O. Box 45245
Nairobi

KOREA, REPUBLIC OF
Pan Korea Book Corporation
P.O. Box 101, Kwangwhamun
Seoul

KUWAIT
MEMRB
P.O. Box 5465

MALAYSIA
University of Malaya Cooperative Bookshop Limited
P.O. Box 1127, Jalan Pantai Baru
Kuala Lumpur

MEXICO
INFOTEC
Apartado Postal 22-860
Col. PE/A Pobre
14060 Tlalpan, Mexico D.F.

MOROCCO
Societe d'Etudes Marketing Marocaine
2 Rue Moliere, Bd. d'Anfa
Casablanca

THE NETHERLANDS
InOr Publikaties
Noorderwal 38
7241 BL Lochem

NEW ZEALAND
Hills Library and Information Service
Private Bag
New Market
Auckland

NIGERIA
University Press Limited
Three Crowns Building Jericho
Private Mail Bag 5095
Ibadan

NORWAY
Tanum-Karl Johan, A.S.
P.O. Box 1177 Sentrum
Oslo 1

OMAN
MEMRB Information Services
P.O. Box 1613, Seeb Airport
Muscat

PAKISTAN
Mirza Book Agency
65, Shahrah-e-Quaid-e-Azam
P.O. Box No. 729
Lahore 3

PERU
Editorial Desarrollo SA
Apartado 3824
Lima

THE PHILIPPINES
National Book Store
701 Royal Avenue
Metro Manila

POLAND
ORPAN
Palac Kultury i Nauki
00-901 WARSZAWA

PORTUGAL
Liveria Portugal
Rua Do Carmo 70-74
1200 Lisbon

SAUDI ARABIA, QATAR
Jarir Book Store
P.O. Box 3196
Riyadh 11471

SINGAPORE, TAIWAN, BURMA, BRUNEI
Information Publications
Private, Ltd.
02-06 1st Fl., Pei-Fu Industrial
Bldg., 24 New Industrial Road
Singapore

SOUTH AFRICA
For single titles:
Oxford University Press Southern Africa
P.O. Box 1141
Cape Town 8000

For subscription orders:
International Subscription Service
P.O. Box 41095
Craighall
Johannesburg 2024

SPAIN
Mundi-Prensa Libros, S.A.
Castello 37
28001 Madrid

SRI LANKA AND THE MALDIVES
Lake House Bookshop
P.O. Box 244
100, Sir Chittampalam A. Gardiner Mawatha
Colombo 2

SWEDEN
For single titles:
ABCE Fritzes Kungl. Hovbokhandel
Regeringsgatan 12, Box 16356
S-103 27 Stockholm

For subscription orders:
Wennergren-Williams AB
Box 30004
S-104 25 Stockholm

SWITZERLAND
Librairie Payot
6 Rue Grenus
Case postal 381
CH 1211 Geneva 11

TANZANIA
Oxford University Press
P.O. Box 5299
Dar es Salaam

THAILAND
Central Department Store
306 Silom Road
Bangkok

TRINIDAD & TOBAGO, ANTIGUA, BARBUDA, BARBADOS, DOMINICA, GRENADA, GUYANA, JAMAICA, MONTSERRAT, ST. KITTS AND NEVIS, ST. LUCIA, ST. VINCENT & GRENADINES
Systematics Studies Unit
55 Eastern Main Road
Curepe
Trinidad, West Indies

TURKEY
Haset Kitapevi A.S.
469, Istiklal Caddesi
Beyoglu-Istanbul

UGANDA
Uganda Bookshop
P.O. Box 7145
Kampala

UNITED ARAB EMIRATES
MEMBR Gulf Co.
P.O. Box 6097
Sharjah

UNITED KINGDOM
Microinfo Ltd.
P.O. Box 3
Alton, Hampshire GU 34 2PG
England

VENEZUELA
Libreria del Este
Aptdo. 60.337
Caracas 1060-A

YUGOSLAVIA
Jugoslovenska Knjiga
YU-11000 Belgrade Trg Republike

ZIMBABWE
Textbook Sales Pvt. Ltd.
Box 3799
Harare